THE SUFFOLK COAST AND HEATHS LANDSCAPE

A landscape assessment prepared by Land Use Consultants
for the Countryside Commission, Suffolk County Council,
Suffolk Coastal District Council, Babergh District Council,
Waveney District Council, Essex County Council and
Tendring District Council.

Distributed by:
Countryside Commission Postal Sales
PO Box 124
Walgrave
Northampton NN6 9TL
Tel: 0604 781848

© Countryside Commission 1993
ISBN 0 86170 364 2
CCP 406
Price £7.50

CONTENTS

FIGURES

British Library Cataloguing-in-Publication data.
A catalogue record for this book is available from the British Library.

Cover: *River Alde near Snape* (David Burton Associates)

Designed and produced by Imaging – Cheltenham
Maps produced by The Edge – Cheltenham
Printed by Severnprint Limited – Gloucester

FOREWORD

The Suffolk Coast and Heaths, designated as an Area of Outstanding Natural Beauty (AONB) in 1969, is a special blend of lowland landscapes that has inspired artistic celebration for many years. Wild heathlands, tilled fields and forests combine with marshes, estuaries and a restless coastline to create a subtle beauty that is often slow to reveal itself but which is all the more rewarding for that.

Despite its proximity to London, the area has retained its remoteness and tranquillity. The farmlands, tamed from woodland, heath and marsh over the years; the picturesque villages and towns that add to its charm; and the heritage of churches and other historic buildings are all testament to a long human presence. It is only recently that its increasingly popular appeal has begun to have a significant impact.

This landscape assessment is a timely and essential contribution to the preparation of a management plan for the area by the Suffolk Coast and Heaths Joint Advisory Committee. We are publishing it as a means of raising people's awareness of the natural beauty of the area and its increasing vulnerability.

This report is the 13th in the landscape assessment series. The Countryside Commission will be publishing landscape assessments for a number of other AONBs over the next few years.

SIR JOHN JOHNSON
Chairman
Countryside Commission

PREFACE

This report results from a study undertaken to assess the landscape of the Suffolk Coast and Heaths AONB. The report aims to draw out the special qualities of this landscape, to trace its evolution over the centuries and to identify forces for change that could undermine its character. The broad aims of such an assessment are to raise awareness of the importance of the AONB and to guide those responsible for developing and implementing policies for the area. A separate technical report has also been produced that extends the assessment to associated areas outside the AONB, provides a more detailed examination of management issues and proposes a methodology for monitoring future landscape change in the area.

In carrying out the work, we have been guided by the Countryside Commission's guidelines on landscape assessment [1] and by our experience in carrying out other similar assessments. In essence, the method has involved: desk study of relevant background material, analysis of geology, topography and land cover; consultation with a range of relevant agencies including local authorities, nature conservation bodies and land owners such as the National Trust; field survey; research into both perception of the landscape and forces for change in the landscape; and judgements about the importance of the landscape.

The report sets out our findings, concentrating on the following issues:

- the physical and human influences involved in shaping the landscape;

- a description of the AONB's landscape, ecological and settlement character, including classification of the landscape into a number of recognisable landscape types;

- a review of the forces for change that are influencing the landscape of the Suffolk Coast and Heaths at the present time or that may affect it in the future, together with suggestions as to how management of the AONB can best address these issues;

- information about the way in which the landscape has been perceived and appreciated over the years;

- a summary of the special character and quality of the area that makes it of national importance.

Land Use Consultants
April 1993

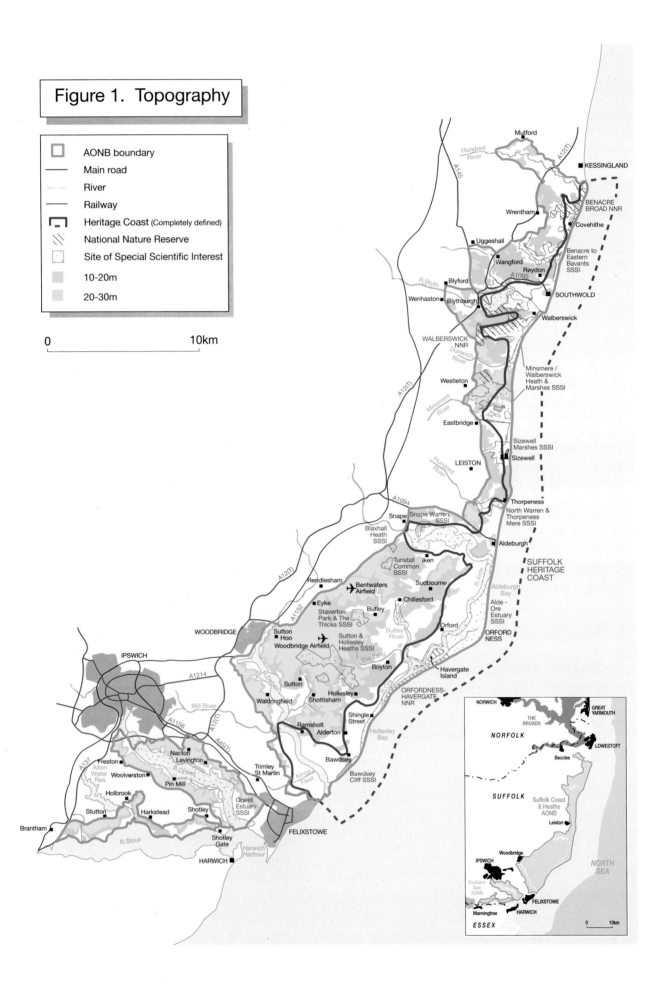

Figure 1. Topography

Legend:
- AONB boundary
- Main road
- River
- Railway
- Heritage Coast (Completely defined)
- National Nature Reserve
- Site of Special Scientific Interest
- 10-20m
- 20-30m

0   10km

The Suffolk Coast and Heaths Area of Outstanding Natural Beauty (AONB) extends from the northern side of the Stour estuary to the east of Ipswich, to as far north as Kessingland (just to the south of Lowestoft) (Figure 1). It covers the wedge of Suffolk that lies between the A12 trunk road and the coast – an area divided by the many estuaries that penetrate inland. This physical landform has, in many ways, been the saviour of the coast and heaths, making the construction of a north-south coast road impossible and preventing the development common along many other stretches of coast. The area has retained a relatively remote and tranquil atmosphere, and gives the impression that many of this century's changes have passed it by. Its towns are refreshingly uncommercialised, much of its coast remains wild and exposed and the landscape is sprinkled with many farms and villages that date back to before the *Domesday* book.

For many visitors, the unique landscape of the Suffolk Coast and Heaths comes as something of surprise. Often they expect this area to share the characteristics of the rolling arable landscapes usually associated with much of East Anglia. But the Suffolk Coast and Heaths are different; the landscape is an intricate mosaic of shingle beaches, crumbling cliffs, marshes, estuaries, heathland, forests and farmland. It is a secret landscape that is slow to reveal itself, its subtle complexity challenging the assumptions that are commonly made about lowland landscapes. Equally, it is a landscape whose mystery encourages and rewards exploration.

Physical influences

The solid geology of the Suffolk Coast and Heaths is comparatively simple and is dominated by rocks formed by sedimentary processes (Figure 2). These soft, generally undisturbed rocks are responsible for creating the area's gently rolling landscape. The coastal strip falls into two parts; north of the Deben the solid geology is predominantly Pleistocene Crags (mainly Red Crag), which consist of marine shelly sands laid down during the Quaternary era. The older Coralline Crag surfaces as a ridge between Orford and Aldeburgh, through which the valleys of the Alde and Butley Rivers have been eroded. To the south of the Deben, the principal underlying rock is London Clay, formed during the Tertiary era.

The soft rocks in this part of East Anglia are seldom visible; outcrops only occur on the Deben, Orwell and Stour estuaries where the Coralline Crag can be seen

The soft rocks of the coast are easily eroded.

as low cliffs such as that at Ramsholt on the Deben. The much older chalk deposits that underlie the whole area have only been exposed in the Orwell Estuary where dredging of the river channel to Ipswich has cut through the London Clay.

The surface or drift geology of the area has three main elements. The central part of Suffolk is almost entirely covered by Boulder Clay, or Till, formed under ice sheets during the middle and late phases of the last ice age. This clay is mixed with fragments of chalk and flint. Fingers of Till extend towards the coast, their heavy, and poorly drained character contrasting with the light and sandy deposits of glacial outwash gravels that fringe it. These gravels, which are found along the coast away from the river valleys, have had an important influence on the vegetation and landscape of the area. The deposits along river valleys in the area are derived from the underlying sedimentary deposits together with the Boulder clay that covers much of their catchment area.

The soils of the Suffolk Coast and Heaths comprise extensive areas of sandy soil along the coast – forming the 'sandlings'; the loamy soils derived from sands and gravels that prevail south of the River Deben and a number of areas of clay loams derived from the chalky Boulder Clay that lie to the west.

During the Anglian Glaciation, most of East Anglia was covered by ice. As the ice age came to an end, and the ice sheet retreated northwards, so the meltwaters drained east and south east, eroding the river valleys that drain into the North Sea. A continuing combination of subsidence and climatic changes resulted in changing sea-levels that later 'drowned' the river valleys that had been enlarged by the glacial meltwaters, creating the series of estuaries that now characterise the Suffolk coast.

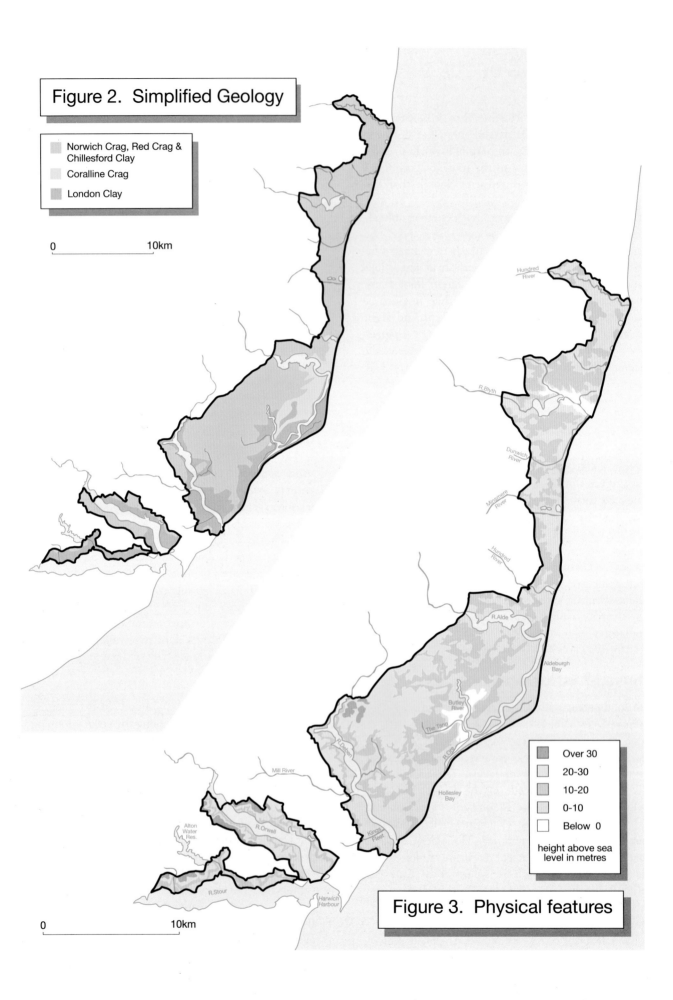

Figure 2. Simplified Geology

Norwich Crag, Red Crag & Chillesford Clay

Coralline Crag

London Clay

0   10km

Figure 3. Physical features

	Over 30
	20-30
	10-20
	0-10
	Below 0

height above sea level in metres

Hundred River

R.Blyth

Dunwich River

Minsmere River

Hundred River

R.Alde

Aldeburgh Bay

Butley River

The Tang

R.Deben

R.Ore

Mill River

Hollesley Bay

Alton Water Res.

R.Orwell

Kings Fleet

R.Stour

Harwich Harbour

0   10km

The distinctive landscape of Suffolk's coast is also the product of the related processes of marine erosion and deposition. Several sections of coast, for instance that near Dunwich, comprise cliffs made of the sandy and shelly crag described above. These friable rocks are easily eroded and in places have been known to crumble into the sea at the rate of 20 m/yr.

Erosion of Suffolk's crumbling cliffs is paralleled by deposition of the shingle beaches that characterise much of the coastline. These beaches are often steep and shelved like the one at Aldeburgh, echoing the stormy waves that shift the shingle along the coast.

Orford Ness, the most dramatic example of this shingle landscape, lies south of Aldeburgh where the process of long shore drift has created a shingle spit over 14 km long. Suffolk Wildlife Trust [2] estimate that, during the last 800 years, the Ness has grown at an average of 12 m/yr, diverting the river Alde/Ore southwards, parallel to the coast, and cutting off the once prosperous port of Orford from the open sea. Shingle deposition elsewhere has sealed the mouths of a number of rivers and estuaries with shingle bars, some of which are periodically breached, or suffer serious erosion during the most severe storms. It is likely that such occurrences will become more frequent as global warming results in rising sea-levels and increasing frequency and severity of storms.

The combination of geology and the physical processes that have modified it, has produced a gentle landscape comprising a series of estuaries and broads that dissect a gently-rolling plateau that rarely climbs much beyond 30 m above sea-level. Figure 3 illustrates the subtle nature of the landform.

Human influences

Prehistoric

It is now thought that, following the last ice age, forest covered virtually the whole of modern day Suffolk, including those areas along the coast that remain as heath today or that have been 'reclaimed' for arable agriculture during the last few centuries. It is likely that this woodland was a mixture of birch and pine, with mixed oak forest becoming more common as the climate became warmer.

With the introduction of agriculture during the Neolithic era (4,600 BC and 2,700 BC), humans began to have a significant influence on the landscape through forest clearance to grow crops and graze livestock. Evidence in the form of Neolithic pottery indicates that in eastern Suffolk these farmers tended to settle first in areas of light soil and along river valleys.

The clearance of woodland during the Neolithic period is significant because it began the process that created the areas of heathland that are so much a part of the landscape of the Suffolk Coast and Heaths. The clearance of woodland continued through the Bronze and Iron Ages, stimulated by population growth and facilitated by better tools.

The forest that had developed on the poor sandy soils was in a delicately balanced equilibrium, with nutrients being cycled to maintain the fertility of the acid brown-earth soils. The felling of the trees and the subsequent cultivation upset this equilibrium. Without modern techniques of irrigation and fertilisation, the light soils quickly lost their nutrients and were transformed to an acid podsol on which heather flourishes but is poorly suited to cultivation. Faced with falling yields of crops, the early farmers moved on to newly cleared areas nearby. In this way the forests of the Suffolk coast were gradually cleared and replaced by extensive heathland stretching from Ipswich to Lowestoft.

The Romans

The transformation of the Suffolk landscape continued with the arrival of the Romans in the first century AD. More areas were brought into cultivation, settlement patterns changed and a trading culture was introduced. For the first time a series of larger settlements developed at the intersection of Roman roads, operating as markets and distribution centres for the surrounding countryside. Such small 'towns' included those established at Wenhaston close to the River Blyth, at Felixstowe and at Knodishall. Other Roman settlement appears to have been limited to a large number of smaller settlements, most probably small farms and peasant homesteads and these tended to be concentrated along the river valleys. The precise course of Roman roads in east Suffolk have not been preserved, but they probably included much of what is now the A12 together with some east–west roads.

Anglo Saxons

Considerable uncertainty surrounds the end of the Roman era in the 5th century AD. Although large areas that had been settled appear to have lost their population, there is little evidence of the violent upheaval traditionally associated with the Anglo Saxon invasion. However, there is evidence that the spread of cultivation into clay areas ceased or went into reverse, with farming shrinking back to the lighter, more easily cultivated soils found in the east and north west of the county. Most evidence about this period comes from a series of cemetery sites, the most dramatic of which is at Sutton Hoo, where up to 17 burial mounds have been identified, including one that was probably a royal grave and was found to contain the remains of a long ship together with a wealth of grave goods. A similar, if smaller, ship was discovered in a burial mound at Snape, further north.

Although Christianity had died out at the end of the Roman period, it was re-introduced into East Anglia during the first part of the 7th century. This resulted in changing patterns of settlement, with some farms and villages being abandoned, and others developing around churches.

Domesday

The *Domesday* book gives a picture of the Suffolk landscape at the end of the first millennium. The similarity between the landscapes of 1086 and of the present day is striking, lending weight to the argument that the county's landscape is ancient. The record shows that four out of five of Suffolk's medieval churches were already in existence, most being constructed of wood (to be replaced by stone buildings in later centuries). The majority of these churches exist today and are striking features of the landscape.

The often isolated locations of many of these churches, eg those at Butley and Mutford, has led people to suggest that surrounding villages may have been abandoned, perhaps as a consequence of the Black Death. However, there is rarely any evidence of such villages and some observers argue that the scattered pattern of churches is the result of groups of farmers jointly paying for a new church and selecting a mutually convenient location.

Domesday gives the impression of a stable society with watermills established on many of the rivers and saltpans around the coast. The period of greatest forest clearance had come to an end and the heaths had become an essential element of medieval society and economy. *Domesday* recorded, for example, that sheep, cattle, pigs and even bee-hives were kept on Leiston Common. Gorse, or furze, was used to fuel village bread ovens, bracken for animal bedding and thatch and heather for mattresses, walling, medicinal infusions and even ale making. The turf of the heaths was cut and dried for use as fuel. The commons also fulfilled a social function, serving as a meeting place and the location for village fairs, public meetings and other events.

The Norman Conquest heralded a series of important changes for the landscape of eastern Suffolk. Among the most significant was the introduction of the manorial system. The Norman Lords were quick to enclose large areas of common heathland for their sheep to graze and although villagers retained their commoners' rights, it was for a much reduced area. The Normans also introduced rabbits that colonised the

heaths and played an important role in preventing invasion by scrub, until the 1950s when the population was devastated by myxomatosis. The names of several heaths in the AONB reflect the importance of rabbits, including Snape Warren and North and South Warrens near Aldeburgh.

This period saw the growing use of stone in building construction. Timber churches were gradually replaced and a series of castles built as a means of reinforcing the power of the new ruling class. There were relatively few such castles in the area, the best surviving example being the one at Orford.

The period also saw the growing influence of religious orders in Suffolk, with many parishes containing monastic landholdings. The remains of a number of the abbeys and priories of this period may still be seen, for instance at Leiston, Dunwich and Butley. Several towns and villages were granted Royal licence to hold markets, the most significant and longstanding being those at Blythburgh (recorded in *Domesday*), Orford, Aldeburgh, Dunwich and Southwold. By the early 14th century Dunwich had developed as an important port, equal in size to the town of Norwich.

The Middle Ages

This period witnessed the growing importance of the Suffolk coastal ports for shipbuilding, fisheries, and trade. Aldeburgh was an important centre for trade, shipbuilding and fishing. The town originally had a harbour on its northern side, but like many of the bays and estuaries along this part of the coast, the build up of shingle and the use of larger ships rendered it redundant by the end of the 16th century. By the 17th century the shipbuilding industry had gone into decline, largely as a consequence of the scarcity of local timber. Writing in 1603, Robert Ryece [3] commented that buildings and ship building "hath almost consumed our timber" but that there was little concern to plant new trees.

Although the process of enclosure is normally associated with Parliamentary Acts of the 18th and 19th centuries, in Suffolk there was a phase of enclosure during the Middle Ages as landowners sought to increase their acreage of pasture and arable land. The period marked the beginning of the process that has gradually eroded the heaths throughout the AONB and that has drained the marshes fringing its rivers and estuaries.

Land owners, keen to extend their pasture lands came into conflict with local people who defended the common land on which their livelihoods depended. Lee Chadwick [4] describes this process as a "continuous tug of war at village level between the owner of the soil and the owner of these common

In the Middle Ages the coast grew in importance for ship building and fishing, and coastal ports thrived.

rights". Faced with the loss of commons, many peasants took the law into their own hands, sometimes smashing new fences and gates at night.

The drainage of marsh represents one of the most significant changes that man has effected on the landscape of the Suffolk coast. In an area of poor sandy soils, the marsh drainage represented a means of exploiting the extremely fertile alluvial sediment. Among the largest areas of marsh drainage took place along the Alde/Ore south of Aldeburgh, where the reclamation of Sudbourne and Gedgrave Marshes has pushed the river into a narrow channel, constrained between high flood walls. Arnott [5] describes the early drainage along this section of river:

> "Walls to protect the lantern marshes appear to have been built about 1600. They must have been erected by men who knew their job, who carefully selected and aligned the site, graded the drains at the back to work with the tidal sluices at the front. They must have known of the durability and binding quality of the coarse grass

which covers the banks and which will outlast the concrete slabs so beloved of our present-day experts."

In the Blyth estuary approximately 1,100 ha of marsh and mudflat had been reclaimed by 1842, though some 250 ha have since returned to mudflats. Taking all the estuaries together, the Suffolk Wildlife Trust [2] estimates that 10,800 ha of marsh and mudflat have been reclaimed, compared with about 4,300 ha that remain today.

The 18th and 19th centuries

Since much of Suffolk's agricultural land had been enclosed during previous centuries, the effect of 18th and 19th century enclosure was concentrated in areas of heath and common. Writing in 1794, Arthur Young [6] reflected the commonly held view that these heathlands were a wasted resource. He had previously applauded the way that "capital converted barren heathland into smiling cornfields". Today, evidence of former areas of heathland remain in the form of place names incorporating the words 'walks' (derived from sheep walks), 'warren', or 'common'. For commoners, the enclosure of heathland represented a further erosion of their livelihood as areas of common grazing disappeared and fuel and other goods had to be paid for. For many, the enclosure of heathland also represented a cultural loss. It certainly resulted in the loss of a traditional way of life and the erosion of a landscape that, where it remains today, contributes so much to the character of the area.

The Napoleonic Wars further hastened the reclamation as corn prices rose. The Wars also led to the construction of the Martello Towers along the coast between Felixstowe and Aldeburgh from 1808. Although their military role soon passed, they continued to be used by the Inland Revenue who tried to control the centuries-old practice of smuggling, and by coastguards who watched the treacherous coast.

The 18th and 19th centuries saw progressive improvements in transport and the area became an increasingly popular location for large country houses. These were usually sited along the sides of the larger river estuaries, particularly along the Stour and Orwell, where they could command fine views along the river. Shotley Peninsula, for example, has several large houses and halls, some dating back to the 16th century. Many of the larger estates incorporated significant areas of woodland, often in the form of shelter- belts, representing an important element in the estuarine landscape.

The 20th century

Farming has traditionally been one of the principal agents for change in the landscape of the Suffolk Coast and Heaths. The 20th century has seen the pace of change quicken as farmers have been encouraged to intensify and expand production. The changes that have taken place in this century have had a serious effect on the landscape.

During the Second World War, and in the period since the war, farmers were encouraged to increase production. In the river valleys and estuaries improvements in land drainage linked to the introduction of enhanced sea defences and flood protection, allowed former marshland and wet pasture to be converted either to dry pasture, or frequently to arable land.

Such changes have continued over recent years, eg it has been estimated that the grassland area in the whole of the AONB fell by 32 per cent between 1970 and 1981. One of the consequences of these changes has been the breakdown of the traditional pattern of landscape features, especially in the estuaries.

Farming has traditionally been one of the principal agents for change in the landscape of the Suffolk Coast and Heaths.

Traditionally this landscape was characterised by salt-rich marsh and wet grassland in the valley bottom next to the river. This was edged by a strip of trees or woodland, often on poorer soils or steep ground at the break of slope, separating the marsh from the drier sandy soils and arable fields on the valley sides and the sandlings above. Where intensification has been extreme this pattern has been eroded by the following sequence of change.

First, the construction of flood embankments created damp rather than wet pasture or marsh. Improvements in drainage then lowered the water table and created dry pasture. Improved soil conditions allowed the pasture to be ploughed and converted to arable right up to the valley side. Neglect and eventual removal of the line of woodland at the foot of the slope have created large fields that sweep down across the valley slopes and floor, masking the separate identity of the former marsh and grazing land in the valley.

On the sandlings, intensification in this century has continued to lead to reclamation of large areas of heathland for agriculture. Economies of scale and the use of large machinery have encouraged farmers to grub out hedges and amalgamate fields here and on the valley sides. The light, sandy soils are not naturally highly fertile, do not retain moisture and are prone to erosion by high winds, often collecting in drifts along roads. Cultivation of crops on this land has therefore required high levels of fertiliser application and irrigation.

Such intensive agriculture has had a number of consequences for the landscape. The most significant include the loss of structural features such as hedges, ditches, banks, copses and lines of trees. Irrigation equipment, including pipes, hose reels, and irrigation booms, sometimes of enormous size sufficient to cover whole fields, are often highly visible and eye catching. New developments, such as the use of plastic sheeting to protect crops and conserve moisture, can also dramatically change the agricultural scene. New, large machinery often requires special provision for storage, so large, often 'industrial' style, agricultural buildings have been built close to more traditional farmsteads or in open fields. They can be intrusive and certainly bear little resemblance to the local vernacular style of farm buildings, which are characteristic of the area.

Changes in both crops and farming methods have also had an effect on the landscape. Alterations in price support and subsidies under the EC Common Agricultural Policy (CAP) have led to changes in crops in the area. Recently there have been notable increases in flax production, which many regard as a positive influence on the landscape because of the delicate blue flowers of the plant. Another notable change has been the expansion of open-air pig farming. Although many applaud the introduction of more humane farming practices, overgrazed fields and rows of metal pig-shelters often have a negative effect on the landscape.

Afforestation of heathland has also brought major changes to the landscape this century. The early decades saw the establishment of three major coniferous forests by the Forestry Commission on former heathland at Rendlesham, Tunstall and Dunwich. These forests provoke mixed opinions. While it cannot be denied that the replacement of large areas of heathland with a monoculture of coniferous trees meant the loss of important features and habitats, the forests have become important landscape features in their own right, adding structure and character to the area of the sandlings. They complement the many shelter-belts and coverts and contrast with the adjoining mosaic of heathland and farmland.

A variety of other large-scale developments have occurred within the AONB, many of them pre-dating the special designation of the area. Suffolk's strategic position meant that the county played an important role during the Second World War. Even today fields along the coast are littered with concrete pill boxes, and at places like Bawdsey more substantial gun emplacements, watchtowers and other coastal defences still remain. During the war, Orford Ness was used as a site for military research and the masts that remain are now used to broadcast the BBC World Service.

The most significant war-time developments were the two military airbases that lie within the AONB – Bentwaters Airfield near Rendlesham, and Woodbridge Airfield built in Rendlesham Forest. These have continued to operate since the war, and are prominent in the landscape, with their watertowers and aircraft hangers often visible above the trees. However, their visual impact is greatest at night when they are brightly lit and stand out sharply in contrast to the dark countryside around them.

In the 1950s the small fishing village of Sizewell was chosen as the site for the sixth of Britain's nuclear power stations. Sizewell 'A' was commissioned in the 1960s, a second reactor, Sizewell 'B' is currently under construction, and a third, a twin reactor is proposed by Nuclear Electric. The huge, rectangular block of Sizewell 'A' and the equally large sphere of Sizewell 'B' have a very intrusive impact on the surrounding landscape. The low profile of the coast together with the vast bulk of the buildings means that they are visible from as far north as Lowestoft and as far south as Aldeburgh. The lines of electricity pylons marching across the countryside towards Sizewell also have a major detrimental impact on the landscape.

The huge bulk of Sizewell power station is visible from a wide area.

Developments outside but visible from within the AONB have also had a significant impact on the character of the landscape. The northern boundary of the AONB, for example, runs along the edge of Kessingland where a static caravan park spills down the hillslope next to the sea. More serious impacts are associated with the dock facilities at Harwich and Felixstowe. Felixstowe Docks have recently expanded west along the north shore of the Orwell, crossing into the AONB. The large cranes, gantries, sheds and other facilities of both these ports are clearly visible from the shores of the Stour and the Orwell, particularly when lit at night, and contrast with the otherwise undeveloped character of these estuaries.

The special character of the Suffolk Coast and Heaths and its wealth of wildlife mean that it has long been popular with visitors, although it has managed to resist the commercial over-development often found in other popular coastal areas. Recreation has nevertheless had an effect on the landscape, most obviously in the form of car parks, traffic, caravan parks, visitor centres and cafés, signs, hides and litter. Individually, these usually have a comparatively small impact, but taken as a whole they are a visible reminder of the balance that must be struck between conservation and public access and enjoyment.

Figure 4. Landscape types

Sandlings with agriculture
Sandlings with woodland
Sandlings with heathland
River valley
Drained coastal marsh
Coastal marsh
Estuary valley slopes
Estuary with drained marsh
Estuary with marsh
Estuary river & mudflats
Coast with shingle beaches

0   10km

Hundred River
R.Blyth
Dunwich River
Minsmere River
Hundred River
R.Alde
Aldeburgh Bay
Butley River
R.Deben
Hollesley Bay
Mill River
Alton Water Res.
R.Orwell
R.Stour
Harwich Harbour

The character of the Suffolk Coast and Heaths is the product of both physical and human influences. Much of the quality of the landscape rests on the great diversity of landscape elements occurring throughout the area in varying combinations and locations. The landscape as a whole is characterised by coastal and estuarine features such as cliffs, shingle beaches, marshes and meres; the contrasting heathland, forests and farmland of the sandlings; the rich flora and fauna; and the typical buildings and settlements; and the area's great houses and designed landscapes.

Landscape character

In simple terms, the landscape can be divided into five broad categories namely: the coast, the estuaries, coastal marsh, river valleys and the sandlings. Within each of these categories, it is possible to distinguish a number of individual landscape types (described below), which have a distinct and relatively homogeneous character. There are also, of course subtle differences within each of the landscape types, some of which are referred to in the descriptions. In particular, each estuary is described in turn. It must be remembered that the descriptions of landscape types are generalised and that the boundaries between types, illustrated in Figure 4, often indicate transitions rather than marked changes on the ground.

Coast

Unlike other stretches of the British coast, Suffolk's shoreline is, for the most part, undeveloped and uncommercialised. The boundaries formed by the estuaries cutting inland has isolated the intervening areas of sandling. It has never been practical to build a road on this most dissected shoreline, and access to the sea remains difficult. The only section of coast road runs the few kilometres between Aldeburgh and Thorpeness. Development has tended to be concentrated in historic towns, at the heads of the estuaries or strung along the coast. The land and coast between these settlements lies isolated and relatively undisturbed.

The Suffolk coast does not share the drama and grandeur of cliffs or huge expanses of sandy beach for which other counties are renowned. It is a subtle landscape of low crumbling cliffs and steep, unremitting shingle beaches, a subtlety echoing that of the estuaries and the areas inland. The coast sweeps in a series of wide bays, punctuated by landmarks; lighthouses, church towers and the Napoleonic Martello Towers break the skyline. Sizewell's nuclear power stations are another landmark, but one that conflicts with the understated character of the surrounding landscape.

The footpath running the length of the Suffolk coast follows the tidal defence embankments that fringe the drained marshes. It runs along the steep shingle beaches and 'nesses' that have closed the mouths of former estuaries, along cliffs topped with fields, forest and heaths, and through the seaside towns such as Southwold and Aldeburgh. The coast can be divided into two main landscapes: shingle beaches and cliffs.

Shingle beaches

For the most part, the Suffolk coast is made of shingle beaches. These are not shallow, expansive beaches, but steeply raked banks of pebbles, heaped up into shelves and terraces by successive storms and the daily pattern of the tides. The pebbles themselves are blue, orange, black and grey, giving the beaches a warm, dappled hue. In many places the beaches have been piled higher than the dry land behind, mirroring the tidal defences found elsewhere and giving views over marsh or farmland as well as out to sea. However, the ability of the sea to move and shape the shingle is greatest at Orford Ness where the process of long shore drift has piled up a broad, snaking pebble spit over 14 km long, its arm enclosing the curve of the River Ore.

The Suffolk beaches are open and exposed. Views inland are quickly obscured by the height of the pebble bank, and one faces the expanse of the sea. On calm, sunny summer's days these beaches are warm and

Many of the steeply raked and terraced shingle beaches are popular with the dedicated fishermen.

hospitable, the most accessible ones littered with sunbathers, but with a grey sky and a sharp easterly wind, they can be harsh and desolate. Imogen Holst [7] described them:

> "On a stormy day, even in summer, the grey sea batters itself against the shelf, dragging the shingle down with a scrunching, grating, slithering sound. To anyone who lives on the Suffolk coast, this sound means home."

At aptly named Shingle Street and Aldeburgh, houses and other buildings appear to rise up out of the shingle bank, adding a slightly surreal quality. In other places, the beach is strewn with the stubby boats used by local fishermen, and small sheds squat above the high water mark, housing the fishermen's capstans or winches. The shingle beaches are a favourite with sea fishermen who can be seen in most weathers, day and night sheltering under their huge green umbrellas, attention focused on their fishing lines.

Cliffs

Suffolk's soft rocks are quickly eroded by the waves of the North Sea that constantly batter the coast. Nowhere is the power of these waves more obvious than where there are cliffs. The resulting landscape is one of constant change, with debris piled at the base of the crumbling cliffs while blocks of masonry and tree stumps litter the beach below.

The cliffs themselves are low and crumbly, composed of the sandy, orange-brown crags that predominate along the coast. In places, grasses and other plants have colonised the piles of eroded soil and soft rocks, and occasionally a tree sits on the cliff edge, inclined at a precarious angle, waiting for the next storm to sweep it away. Hammond Innes [8] described the scene at Dunwich:

> "To get the impact of a land under constant attack you need to go to Dunwich and see the old brown bones of the dead poking out of low crumbling cliffs, and if the day is rough, listen for the tolling bells of churches fallen into the sea."

The sea's encroachment is also evident from the top of the cliffs. At Covehithe and Easton Bavents, for example, the severed ends of roads and tracks hang in mid-air above the cliff face, and triangular fragments are all that remain of once extensive fields. The constant change of the cliff line is reflected by an unusually large number of dead trees, dying as the groundwater levels fall as the cliff line approaches and by exposure to salt spray. These qualities combine to give an impression of a threatened and somewhat neglected landscape, as farmers and landowners bow to the inevitability of coastal retreat.

Estuaries

In contrast to the exposed coast, the AONB's estuaries provide sheltered and relatively stable landscapes. Each estuary has a distinct character, the product of landform, landcover, settlement or use. Separate descriptions of each estuary included in this section reflect this individuality, drawing out the key features that make each river so special. A common element, however, is the peace and tranquillity found within these estuaries. This quality is most noticeable on the Alde near Snape or along the Deben, but is equally important on working rivers like the Orwell where the clutter of yachts and other pleasurecraft is occasionally overshadowed by the huge container vessels that ply their way to and from the port of Ipswich.

Yet the composition of each estuary's landscape is constantly changing. Each tide creates a series of scenes; at the ebb, the shining mudflats crossed by meandering streams and rivulets are peppered by yachts, often resting at crazy angles, while at high tide, the brimming lake is filled with birds and their calls. The changing light adds a further dimension to this landscape, shimmering on mudflats and reflecting on the water.

The estuaries vary from south to north. The Stour and Orwell are massive and relatively straight, the side slopes rising steeply from a wide expanse of water. Their slopes are often well wooded, with large country houses positioned to enjoy views over the estuary. As one moves north, so the estuarine valleys become shallower, the proportion of land to river increases and the river's more sinuous path is flanked by extensive expanses of flat, drained marsh at the foot of the gently rising valley slopes. Rivers such as the Alde and the Blyth widen inland where flood defences have been allowed to deteriorate and the river flood areas drained for agriculture. The level of boating activity also varies between estuaries. The Orwell and Deben tend to be more popular with sailors, whereas in the northern estuaries, boating is generally limited to the lower reaches of the river, for instance on the Alde at Slaughden and the Blyth at Southwold.

Generally, moored boats tend not to be concentrated in formal marinas or yacht havens, but congregate in apparently random patterns, clustering around riverside villages like Pin Mill and Ramsholt. The interesting collection of craft and the disorganised appearance of their moorings tend to sit comfortably in this gentle, informal landscape. Similarly, jetties and landing stages often appear ramshackle, having grown incrementally over the years, adding a quality to the landscape that more modern marinas do not achieve. However, as Chapter 3 will show, boating and

In peaceful estuaries the shining mudflats are often dotted with boats.

moorings are a sensitive issue since further growth would lead to overcrowding along the estuaries, in turn undermining the quality of these special landscapes.

Estuaries with marsh

As Chapter 1 has described, past pressures to expand agricultural production have meant that many areas of former marsh have been drained. However, the remaining areas of marsh within the Suffolk estuaries help to create the calm and tranquil atmosphere that is characteristic of these broad river valleys. Traditionally, these marshes extend from the inter-tidal zone, where salt tolerant plants can survive, through reed beds to dry land marked by a line of trees.

The extent and character of the marsh varies between the estuaries. In the Stour and Orwell, the marsh is generally confined to the saltings running along the shore below the tidal defence embankment. Here the marsh is made up of clumps of salt-tolerant plants separated by areas of mud or shingle. Occasionally, this marshy strip widens into an area of pools and channels separated by well-established marshland plants, sometimes with reed beds along the edge of dry land.

Other estuaries in the AONB tend to have more extensive areas of marsh, particularly inland, such as on the Butley River where the river is almost lost between the wide beds of swaying reeds. In several places, the flood defences have been allowed to break down and once drained areas are again inundated, reverting to mudflats and marshes. At Snape, for instance, the Alde has reclaimed drained fields, replacing them with glistening mudflats and the stands of reeds that provide such a sublime setting for Snape Maltings. Here the traditional buildings of the Maltings, the concert hall and even the surrounding sculpture contrast superbly with the peaceful reed beds. The atmosphere of these marshes is as much a

Stands of reeds contribute to the Alde's tranquil atmosphere.

consequence of their sounds as of their setting. The sound of the wind in the reeds is complemented by the sound of water, be it the lapping of the river at high tide, or the whisper of water trickling out of the mud at low tide. Added to this is the ever present bird song, signalling the importance of the reed beds as a nesting and feeding ground for a wide range of birds.

Estuaries with drained marsh

Earlier sections have described the process of marsh drainage that began in the Middle Ages reaching its climax during the last century as landowners sought to maximise the return from their land holdings. In places the distinction between former marshland and the valley slopes has been eroded and the line of trees that historically marked the slight bank between the marsh and the valley slope has been removed. As a result large fields sweep down from the valley slopes onto the drained marsh as far as the tidal defences.

It is these areas of drained marsh that come closest to the open landscapes that are often associated with East Anglia. On the lower Deben, for example, huge areas of former marsh extend inland on either side of the river, creating a vast, flat, almost featureless plain, extending to the horizon. On a summer's day, it is the sky that dominates this landscape, either because of the great arc of blue, or more commonly, because of the series of white clouds that stretch across the sky. The land itself lacks hedgerows or trees, the only structure being provided by the drainage channels like the King's Fleet on the Deben and, of course, by the flood defences surrounding them. The river is hidden from these marshes by these flood defences that rise two or three metres above the surrounding land. This has the effect that yachts on the rivers at high tide sail above the level of the surrounding land, appearing as white sails amidst a sea of corn!

Estuary valley slopes

The valley slopes that close the view from the river and its associated areas of marsh or drained marsh are an important part of the estuarine landscape. They form the 'backdrop' to the river landscape, giving it both scale and context. The slopes also represent the transition between the riverine valley base and the inland sandlings areas.

Just as the character of the rivers themselves vary between estuaries, so do those of the valley slopes. The Stour and Orwell estuaries are well defined – the rivers wide, the band of marshes narrow, and the valley slopes comparatively steep. In places the junction of marsh and valley slope is marked by one of the low cliffs that occur at points along these estuaries. Woods play an important role in these two estuaries, particularly along the Orwell where large riverside houses like those at Freston Park and Orwell Park have quite extensive woods or shelter-belts that sometimes extend down to the water's edge. These combine to give the Orwell estuary a well-wooded appearance that contrasts with the more open character of some of the other estuaries and the coast.

The valley slopes in the estuaries of the Deben, Butley, Alde and Blyth tend to be more gentle, particularly in their lower reaches. In part this reflects the wider valley, and the more extensive areas of drained or undrained marsh on either bank. It also reflects the more subtle landform in this part of the AONB. Woodland blocks or forest edges on the edge of the sandlings plateau are important, emphasising the subtle slope and defining the edge of the estuary valley. In other places agricultural improvements have resulted in large, open fields that sweep down from the valley slopes onto its floor, creating an open and rather unstructured landscape.

These estuaries also tend to be more sinuous than those of the comparatively straight Stour and Orwell, and the valley slopes combine to form 'interlocking spurs', that contain views along the estuary, often giving the impression that the valley narrows towards its mouth. On the Butley River, for instance, the well-wooded ridge just north of Gedgrave Hall combines with Burrow Hill on the opposite bank to pinch the estuary near its mouth. The effect of these spurs tends to counter the more open landscape resulting from a wider valley and gentler slopes, giving a sense of enclosure and providing a variety of views as one moves along the estuary. These spurs, or promontories, are often wooded. In other cases their defensible location and protection from flooding resulted in them being settled from early times. Blythburgh is probably the best example of such a settlement though others include Ramsholt, Iken and the historic sites at Yarn and Burrow Hills.

The Stour Estuary

The Stour is the greatest of the estuaries along the Suffolk coast, though only the northern shore lies within the AONB. Broad and straight, the river flows through a landscape of a scale that is not found further north. At Holbrook Bay the estuary is over 3 km wide, transformed from a broad expanse of water to a snaking river amidst a vast sea of mud by the ebb of the tide.

The Stour is still a working river. At its mouth, Parkeston Quay peers across the water at its counterpart Felixstowe on the Orwell. At Mistley and Manningtree on the southern side of the Stour, and therefore beyond the southern boundary of the AONB, a collection of boats clutter the foreshore. These are both old trading ports with a mixture of old warehouses and grain refineries that climb the steep escarpment from the water's edge. Mistley still has an operating quay and ships can often be seen there, loading or unloading their cargoes. At Brantham, on the northern shore, also outside the AONB lies a more modern industrial complex.

The slopes of the Stour estuary rise comparatively steeply, limiting the areas of marsh that characteristically fringe the waterside of the Suffolk estuaries. Many of the mudflats, however, are colonised by salt-tolerant plants whose appearance at low tide is green and lush, especially Greenfield Bay. Above the constantly changing riverscape the estuary slopes sweep away; woodland, generally limited to historic estates and large houses, breaks the overall pattern of large, open, rolling fields among which few smaller, hedged fields still survive.

Close proximity to Ipswich and good communications have helped make the Stour a popular location for large houses. At Stutton and Erwarton grand houses command fine views from the northern valley slope. The existence of these estates has helped preserve woodland within the landscape that might otherwise have been cleared to provide more land for agricultural use.

The Stour is still a working river.

The Orwell Estuary

"Whenever I think of the river it is in the summer light of a still evening when the whole radiance of the sinking sun is flung over Nacton woods, and Pin Mill lies clothed in an opalescent purple mist. It is at this hour, and no other, when the river is so naturally itself."

marsh is now drained and used either for arable agriculture or for pasture, but at Trimley the process has been reversed to create a nature reserve close to the river's edge.

The marshland may be restricted to the downstream areas but saltings and mudflats fill the intertidal zone throughout the estuary. The Orwell's extensive mudflats are second only to those of the Stour and at low tide the broad

The new Orwell Bridge dominates the view north along the Orwell as it curves gracefully over the river.

W G Arnott wrote this in 1954 [9] and the Orwell still retains its special appeal. Its "gentle, placid beauty" makes it popular with many people, but particularly sailors who find it "easy to enter with wide reaches for tacking and sheltered anchorages under wooded shores".

The Orwell is often compared with its neighbour the Stour; its valley slopes are equally steep, often lacking an intermediate fringe of marsh at their feet, but the river itself is narrower and turns through a series of gentle meanders on its route to the sea. The Orwell flows between the loosely-wooded slopes and parkland of historic houses interspersed with rolling farmland and hamlets. Articulating this landscape are small streams that cut into steep, narrow valleys and drain the higher ground. At Nacton and Freston these streams have been dammed to form ornamental pools or lakes, which may have originally been mill pools.

Downstream the valley broadens, opening out to its confluence with the Stour. Here the river is bordered by low, wide expanses of marsh – Shotley Marshes to the south and Trimley Marshes to the north. Much of this extensive

shining expanse teems with birds who gorge themselves on the rich invertebrate life.

The river landscape changes imperceptibly, but continuously, throughout its length. This of all the estuaries, is a river popular with sailors. Yachts and dinghies abound, whether packed into orderly rows in the marinas at Levington and Woolverstone, or swinging with the tide at their moorings by Pin Mill or Freston. The famous and unique waterside hamlet of Pin Mill has a fascinating character all of its own, the foreshore is littered with a strange collection of craft, from old barges to houseboats and smart yachts, and an old smuggling pub – the Butt and Oyster – dating back to the 16th century. From time to time the yachts and pleasure craft are dwarfed by one of the huge container ships that ply their way up and down the river, reminding one that the Orwell is a working river serving the ports of Ipswich at its head, and the modern container port of Felixstowe with its dinosaur-like cranes and gantries near its mouth. The new Orwell Bridge carrying the A12 trunk road, dominates the view north, forming a gateway to Ipswich.

The Deben Estuary

The Deben estuary marks the change from the big southern rivers to the more intimate scale of those in the north of the AONB. The river itself is narrower and far more twisting than the Orwell or the Stour, and the valley shallower and proportionately wider. Occasionally, as at Ramsholt, the river curves around a small promontory, cutting a cliff into the soft red crag.

Curiously, the river and its valley narrow towards its mouth, pinched between ridges running parallel to the coast. Here the coast wraps round into the estuary; the sea forming the distant horizon and banks of shingle swing round into the river mouth. However, it is the stillness and slow pace that distinguish this estuary and have made it a favourite among locals and visitors alike.

At Woodbridge, water slides serenely between its muddy banks, overseen from Sutton Hoo, where the wooded valley rises to the burial place of the Saxon kings.

In spite of its notorious shingle bar and shifting channels, the Deben is popular with sailors. Villages such as Waldringfield, Martlesham Creek and Ramsholt hidden along its shores may be picked out by the clusters of boats anchored midstream.

The fringe of countryside around the river at Woodbridge is quiet, but it is downstream on the marshes that there is a sense of remoteness. Here the fertile land on either side of the river lies flat and open, it stretches unrelieved to its encircling flood defences, which hide the river from view. Between the river and this flat arable plain are squeezed the remnants of once extensive saltings and marsh, although where flood defences break down, as at Hemley, the marsh plants reclaim their place. These lonely marshlands, with their pools, muddy trickling streams, dense reed beds and clamorous birdlife epitomise the natural character of the Deben estuary.

The Alde/Ore Estuary

The River Alde, which becomes the Ore in its lower reaches, is the most unusual of the Suffolk estuaries. From its tidal limit at Snape, the river flows eastward towards Aldeburgh, but before it reaches the sea, it is forced to turn at right angles and flow parallel to the coast, sheltered from the sea by the great shingle bank of Orford Ness. As the Ore emerges from behind the Ness it is joined by the smaller Butley River before finally reaching the sea near Shingle Street.

In its upper reaches, the river flows in a series of broad meanders, curving around low promontories that extend into the mudflats. At Iken cliff, the southern shore rises steeply from the river. A ragged line of old flood defences straggles across the mud towards the Maltings, behind it land that was hard won from the river submits again to the tide and is reclaimed by reeds. To the east the landmark tower of Iken Church appears through trees, now ragged from the 1987 storm. The quiet of the estuary is broken by the stirring of reeds in the wind, bird cries from the mudflats and the whisper of water as the tides rise and fall. This is a serene, almost spiritual place; the atmosphere befitting the site of one of the first monasteries.

Below Iken the Alde estuary broadens out, and the river is flanked by wide, flat areas of drained marsh. Southwards, low promontories, scattered with woodland coverts, extend through the marsh to the river, behind them lies the distant wooded horizon of Tunstall. Yarn Hill stands alone on the edge of the marsh, facing the wide sweep of the river, its low dome defined by a dense thatch of pines. A slight ridge running north eastward to Cowton divides this inland estuary landscape from the coast.

Downstream between the flood defences, which hide Sudbourne Marshes, and the steeply banked shingle of Orford Ness, the Alde becomes the Ore. Along the Ness the view is dominated by a series of radio masts and their associated buildings and at night by the essential lighthouse.

Flowing south, the Ore surrounds the whale-shaped Havergate Island, before being joined by the Butley; a secretive river concealed between extensive reed beds at its head and all-encompassing flood defences that protect the broad, flanking, arable marshes downstream. A white sail above the dyke is often the only clue to the river's presence.

The Blyth Estuary

"This is the valley of the Blyth. The stream ripples and glances over its brown bed warmed with sunbeams; by its bank the green flags wave and rustle, and, all about the meadows shine in pure gold of buttercups... There above rises the gorse, and beyond if I walk for an hour or two, I shall come out upon the sandy cliffs of Suffolk..." [11]

The history of marshland drainage can be clearly traced in the estuary of the River Blyth. In the lower part of the valley, the Blyth is closely contained by the flood defences that protect Southwold's Town Marshes, Reydon and Tinker's Marshes. Southwold stands on a hill on the northern side of the river, its church tower, lighthouse and watertower standing as reference points on the horizon. Facing it, on a low promontory, lies the picturesque village of Walberswick. Between the two, at the mouth of the river, in such contrast with the ordered nature of the town, is Southwold harbour where a ramshackle collection of jetties, huts and sheds serves a variety of boats and yachts. The clutter of wooden buildings does not conflict with the underlying quality of the landscape, as its informal and incremental appearance tends to underline the informal, uncommercialised character of this part of the coast.

The river turns a corner just inland of Tinker's Marsh, and suddenly opens up into a vast expanse of mudflats. These are former areas of marsh, at one time drained for agricultural use, but whose flood defences have deteriorated and whose fields flood once more. As along the Alde, the lines of the old flood defence embankments are sometimes visible as a straggling line crossing the mud, in one case punctuated by the remains of telegraph poles. This broad, muddy meander is contained by wooded slopes to the north and south, but is dominated by Blythburgh that sits on a low promontory extending out into the valley. The village's magnificent church stands on the highest ground, its tower visible for miles around. It is at Blythburgh that the busy A12 crosses the valley of the Blyth, introducing a discordant element into a landscape that is otherwise quiet and still. Above Blythburgh, the river once again contracts, contained between flood defence embankments that protect the drained marsh on either side.

Blythburgh sits on a low promontory overlooking the estuary, its church tower visible for miles around. In this part of the estuary, the Blyth has reclaimed drained marsh where flood defences have been allowed to break down.

Coastal marsh

Distinct from those areas of marshland within the river estuaries are a series of coastal marshes in the northern part of the AONB. Examples include Benacre Broad, Easton Broad and Minsmere. These are former estuaries that have been sealed by the accretion of shingle bars across their mouths. Topographically, they are usually well-contained, bounded by ridges rising to the north and south, and by slopes or woods inland. They form broad, marshy bays separated from the sea by high shingle beaches.

These marshes are dominated by reed beds, usually associated with a pool or broad sited just behind the shingle bar. In some places, the rushes are still cut as material for thatching. The progression from water, through marsh to drier ground, and then the slight rise that marks the lower edge of the valley slopes is easily visible in the changes of vegetation. Reed beds thrive in the wettest areas, but give way to more diverse species as ground conditions become drier. In places, where there has been inappropriate management, the reed beds are tending to dry out, being replaced by drier species and scrub. As the valley side is reached, so a fringe of trees and scrub usually marks the rise in ground level. At Benacre and Easton Broads this has been augmented by plantation woodland that has been established around the marsh, particularly inland where reeds colonise the tributaries running into the marsh, forming fingers extending into the woodland. These woods frame and contain views over the marsh, often limiting them to viewpoints such as the shingle beach or, in the case of Easton Broad, the road that crosses the marsh on a causeway at Potter's Bridge.

In other cases, the woods that surrounded the marsh have been lost, and arable fields now extend to the edge of the reed beds, opening up the landscape, but removing the structural elements that are so important in this gently understated landscape.

Drained coastal marsh

Several of the coastal marshes have been wholly or partially drained to provide land for pasture or arable production. The stretch of land between Aldeburgh and Thorpeness, for example, would once have been coastal marsh, but today extensive pastures lie behind the steep shingle beach, and the reed beds are now confined to drainage ditches that surround the fields. However, the RSPB is undertaking a project to restore this area to marsh. Drained coast marshes are often flat, featureless landscapes that share the same open, exposed atmosphere as their undrained counterparts.

River valleys

Most of the rivers in the Suffolk Coast and Heaths AONB take the form of estuaries, and in most cases, the transition to the river valleys landscape takes place at or beyond the AONB's western boundary. However, there are a number of exceptions, most notably the Hundred River valley in the north, and the upper part of the River Blyth, which although tidal, is very different from the broad estuary downstream.

The river valleys are a small-scale pastoral landscape.

These river valleys have a landscape distinct from those found in the estuaries, coastal marshes or in the sandlings. The overall impression is a pastoral one, with the base of the valley, formerly marsh, drained to create lush pasture for grazing cattle. The river itself is not a prominent feature, often being little more than a broad stream hidden behind shallow flood defences, perhaps marked by an occasional clump of silvery willow or poplar trees. In places the river channel is wide enough for a fringe of reeds to grow, in others, lilies populate the slow moving river, and ducks and swans feed along its course. Hedgerows are few, and the valley bottom is structured by the series of ditches that drain the pasture, and the line of trees along the bottom of the valley slope.

The scale of the valley landscape is, however, very different from the huge expanses of drained marsh found in the river estuaries. Here the base of the valley is comparatively narrow, perhaps extending a few hundred metres either side of the river before the drier valley slopes rise to meet the sandlings. The small sense of scale is emphasised by the valley's meanders that often contain the view up or downstream. The valley slopes tend to be dotted with churches, villages and farmsteads, and are given over to arable cultivation or woods.

Sandlings

Between the river valleys and estuaries lie areas of light, sandy soils that forms a plateau between 20 m and 30 m above sea-level. It is these areas, known locally as the 'sandlings' that once formed the extensive tract of heathland stretching from Ipswich to Lowestoft. The pressure to increase agricultural production during the last 200 years has brought the greater part of the sandlings into cultivation, while large areas of heathland have also been lost to afforestation and to the military airbases at Bentwaters and Woodbridge.

Sandlings with heathland at Westleton Heath.

However, remnants of heathland still survive throughout the AONB and it is becoming an increasingly valued landscape and semi-natural habitat. Recent decades have seen a range of initiatives to ensure that these remaining areas of heath are properly managed and, where opportunities arise, heathland is being re-created. Perhaps the most ambitious is the RSPB's scheme to re-create heathland on arable farmland adjoining their Minsmere reserve.

Extensive woodland cover, either in the form of forests or, more frequently, the shelter-belts and mixed woodland blocks planted by landowners, mean that for the most part views across this gently rolling or flat landscape are contained and structured. However, a number of structures such as church towers, water towers, electricity pylons and masts do rise above the surrounding landscape and can often be seen over a considerable distance. The effect of the 1987 storm has been to open up new vistas, particularly of the airbases that were previously concealed by trees.

The landscape of the sandlings can be divided into three principal types; heathland, forest and agriculture, as described below. However, the character and value of the sandlings landscape is the product of the association of all three landscape types; both in the contrasts between them and in the complex mosaic that results.

Sandlings with heathland

Heathland is similar to a number of other landscapes within the AONB inasmuch as it is only during the latter part of this century that its true value both in terms of landscape and nature conservation has become commonly recognised and steps taken to ensure its protection.

The heathland landscape has a rough, almost wild character with wide expanses of heather and acid grassland peppered with gorse, broom and birch. These heaths provide a stark contrast with the ordered appearance of the surrounding agricultural landscape. The landscape changes with the seasons but is most dramatic in the late summer when the heather blooms creating an undulating bed of purple bushes, contrasting with the flaming yellow flowers of the gorse. Often, as on Westleton Heath, the heathland is bordered by woods that frame the views, their branches and leaves combining with the dark heather to give the landscape a subdued and moody atmosphere. Only at Dunwich, however, does heath extend right up to the top of Minsmere Cliffs; a rare example of coastal heath.

The heathland is rich in nature conservation interest, providing nesting and feeding grounds for a wide variety of interesting and often rare birds and supporting a range of reptiles that can be seen sunning themselves on summer days.

Sandlings with woodland

Woodland is an important element in the sandlings landscape. It occurs throughout the area in the form of comparatively small woods, coverts and shelter-belts, many of which are associated with large estates in the area. In places such as Sutton these woods play an important role in structuring the landscape, as elsewhere, giving emphasis to the subtleties of the landform.

Early in this century the afforestation of large parts of the sandlings created Rendlesham, Tunstall and Dunwich Forests. By the 1980s these had grown into mature pine forests, but the ferocious 1987 storm wreaked havoc, flattening most of the trees. The landscape that results is a direct product of that storm, and is made up of large areas where fallen trees have been cleared into long piles, known as wind-rows, and the areas between planted with new trees. Not all the trees were blown down. Here and there a single tree or a line, the outside of the plantation, remains. These trees have been retained as features and it is hoped that with time they will lose their telegraph pole appearance as the increase in light stimulates more lateral growth. In other places blocks of trees remain, and ordered lines of grey trunks are exposed where neighbouring trees used to stand.

The landscape of these forests is a damaged and desolate one, suggestive of images more usually associated with wartime. However, it is a landscape of reconstruction and transition. Although it will take decades to restore the landscape here, the damage caused by the storm has been used as an opportunity to diversify the uses of the forest, increasing the range of habitats within it and encouraging its use for recreation.

Sandlings with agriculture

It has already been noted that a large proportion of the sandlings area has been improved and brought into agricultural use. This improvement has taken a number of forms, including the extensive use of irrigation equipment and chemical fertilisers to raise the productivity of the sandy soil, and the removal of hedgerows to create huge fields. In some places, for instance in the area known as Sutton Walks, west of Woodbridge Airfield, this has created arable 'prairies', which may reflect the economic needs of modern farming, but results in a monotonous landscape of little visual interest. In common with the largest expanses of drained marsh, it is the huge Suffolk sky that adds character and interest to the scene.

However, much of the area still retains a good structure of hedges and woods that, in this flat landscape, have the effect of creating a series of interlinked 'rooms' or areas, adding variety to the landscape. Perhaps the best example of such a landscape is near Sutton, north of the Deben, where a network of mature shelter-belts has created a patchwork of enclosed fields and blocks of heathland. However, Dutch elm disease together with drought and the 1987 storm have resulted in many dead or dying trees throughout the area. These are often visible either singly or in rows along hedges and field boundaries. What cannot be seen, of course, are the many trees that have already been lost and felled, representing a significant reduction in tree cover in the open countryside.

The agricultural landscape of the sandlings varies with the type of farming, and the time of year. Much of the area is used for cereal production, and in summer huge fields of golden corn form a smooth swaying blanket, in late summer giving way to combine harvesters that leave the landscape scattered with round bales of straw. Other crops include flax, its subtle blue flowers looking like shimmering lakes in summer. Another recent addition to the landscape is open-air pig farming with its rows of corrugated metal pig shelters, bales of straw and fields demarcated by electric fences. Often the farming of these pigs is intense, and on such a scale that the quality of the landscape is seriously affected as in the case of fields near Toby's Walks, a little way to the south of Blythburgh.

Ecological character

The varied landscapes of the Suffolk Coast and Heaths AONB provide a rich and diverse range of habitats, including wetland, coast, heath and woodland. The variety and proximity of these different habitats contribute to the area's unique character and ecological value. The importance of nature conservation is reflected in the number of designations such as National Nature Reserves, Sites of Special Scientific Interest (SSSIs) and County Wildlife Sites that apply to areas within the AONB. Agencies such as Suffolk Wildlife Trust, the RSPB and English Nature are very active in the area, between them owning or managing substantial tracts of land and playing an important role in restoring habitats that have been lost in the past.

As shown, the areas of heath, between Ipswich and Lowestoft, represent the remains of once extensive tracts of open heathland. As such, part of their value is derived from their relative scarcity, regionally and nationally. The flora of these heathland areas includes acid grassland and ling and bell heather, which attract a wide range of heathland butterflies. Historically, the diversity of heathland flora has been maintained by grazing. Although few areas of heath are grazed today (a fact reflected in the encroachment of bracken and scrub in some places) the association with sheep lives on in the local names of many of the plants growing on the heaths: shepherd's calendar; shepherd's cress; shepherd's knot and sheep's bit. Heathland animals include fallow and red deer, rabbits, foxes, stoats and weasels, and reptiles such as adders and common lizards. Birds include woodlark, stonechat and nightjar.

The heathlands are remnants of once more extensive tracts of heather and are of great ecological value.

Within the AONB there are a variety of woodland types, ranging from ancient woodland to the large coniferous forests. The ancient woods in the area comprise trees that are well suited to the area's light, sandy soil, including lowland hazel, pedunculate oak, hornbeam and birch. The coniferous plantations are of some ornithological interest since a number of heathland birds, including woodlark and nightjar have extended their range into the forest. They are also used during the winter by rough legged buzzard and hen harriers.

Suffolk's coast includes large areas of shingle beach that where undisturbed, support rare communities of salt-tolerant plants such as sea pea, sea kale and sea holly. Rare invertebrates are often associated with these plants. Further inland, on the dune slack, the shingle is covered with a thin layer of sand, and it grades to acid grassland that supports a range of nationally rare maritime plants. These areas of shingle are of great importance for breeding birds. Orford Ness, for example, provides the habitat for breeding oyster-catchers, ringed plovers, avocets and a colony of about 8,000 pairs of lesser black back gulls and 2,000 pairs of herring gulls.

Although many marshes have been drained and agriculturally improved, the AONB still contains extensive areas of marshland that are rich in both flora and fauna. Some of the most valuable areas of marsh exist where estuary mouths have been sealed by shingle beaches. Benacre and Easton Broads are excellent examples and have been designated SSSIs. The former is also a National Nature Reserve. These marshes often support a range of rare flora, including marsh marigold, bog pimpernel and marsh orchids. This flora provides habitats for aquatic insects, amphibians and even otters, nesting sites for birds such as sedge, reed and grasshopper warblers and hunting grounds for marsh and hen harriers and owls. The marsh at Minsmere has been modified by the RSPB who have created a number of 'scrapes' or pools that also attract wading birds such as avocets. Some areas of former marsh remain as damp, grazing marsh. These provide a valuable extension of birds' feeding grounds and shelter during bad weather. Blythburgh and Ramsholt Marshes, for example, are used by mallard, wigeon and shelduck, and as a breeding ground by redshank, snipe, mallard and swans.

In addition, there are extensive saltings and mudflats that provide a sheltered feeding ground for wading birds such as greenshank, dunlin, green sandpiper, and, of course, the avocet. In winter, up to 18 species of wading bird have been recorded on the River Orwell, with numbers of waders regularly exceeding 10,000. Both the Stour and Orwell are internationally important in this respect. The salt-marsh and reed beds that traditionally fringe the mudflats are a diminishing habitat providing breeding sites for birds such as reed and sedge warblers, and supporting a particular group of plants that have adapted to the high levels of salt.

Settlement character

The ease with which the Suffolk cliffs are eaten away by the waves of the North Sea suggests that good building stone should be rare in this part of Suffolk. This is generally the case, with stone buildings being the exception rather than the rule. The local Coralline Crag is used in only a few instances, for example at Chillesford to build the grey church tower. The clayey septaria, which outcrops along the coast south of Orford, was used in the construction of Orford castle some 800 years ago. What does occur locally however is flint, derived from the underlying chalk and found along the shingle beaches. Many of the churches built to replace the earliest wooden buildings were constructed of flints bound in mortar. The walls of many of these churches, sometimes with round towers like the one at Mutford, are rough, often showing evidence of different phases of building or repair. Later churches are more elaborate, making greater use of

Mutford church, with its round Norman tower, is a good example of flint construction.

imported stone and developing the technique of 'flushwork' which used split, or 'knapped' flints to infill freestone decoration. One of the finest examples of such work is at Blythburgh.

Flushwork and flint building details.

The use of stone was rare for domestic and farm buildings, most early construction being timber framed with wattle and daub infilling. From the 18th century, however, flint was used, both as rubble and as a decorative and protective finish for exterior walls. Render was also used extensively, often being limewashed or painted one of the soft pinks that are so characteristic of this area. In the late 17th century 'pargetting' became fashionable, a technique that used the plaster render to create embossed patterns on the walls of a building.

Although bricks were introduced during the Roman period, it was not until the 16th century that they began to be used in any quantity. At first their use was confined to the grandest buildings, such as Erwarton Hall on the north side of the Stour. The use of brick gradually spread to other types of building, at first being used to construct fireproof chimneys, and later for entire buildings. Many of the villages and towns throughout the area are composed of buildings using the softly hued red bricks set in grey mortar. The transition to brick was parallelled by the move from thatched roofs to the red or shiny black pantiles that are also a characteristic of the area. Today, with the exception of a couple of Victorian revivals, remaining

examples of thatch are comparatively rare, though a number of thatched churches such as the one at Butley survive.

Except where 20th century residential development has led to the growth of settlements, most hamlets and villages in the AONB tend to be small, often comprising little more than a handful of cottages strung along a country lane. The landscape is also peppered with farms with their brick farmhouses and timber barns, sometimes overshadowed by more modern agricultural buildings. In some cases, very old farmhouses have been extended by the addition of more substantial houses built at right angles to the original. A recent trend has been the conversion of redundant agricultural buildings to dwellings.

The largest settlements in the AONB are the series of towns and villages strung along the coast. Each has its own character, but they share an unspoilt, uncommercialised atmosphere. Southwold is a genteel coastal town with many Georgian and Victorian buildings facing onto a series of greens that are said to be a result of a major fire in 1659. This is one of the few places where the beach is sandy, and the small promenade has a row of colourful beach huts and a stubby pier. The town's gleaming white lighthouse, built on one of the greens in the last century, stands as a landmark for miles around, as does the nearby watertower. Further down the coast is Thorpeness, an Edwardian 'holiday village' built in 1910 by the local landowner Glencairn Stuart Ogilvie. Many of the original buildings are black and white wooden houses, and the village includes a watertower disguised as a 'house in the clouds', once replenished with water pumped by the adjacent windmill. Aldeburgh has a different character again, and many of its colourwashed buildings face straight on to the shelving shingle beach. The predominant colours here are the soft red of the Suffolk bricks and the gentle pastels of pink, yellow and blue that are used to paint the stucco of the sea-front houses. The towns buildings, like some of those in Southwold show many Dutch influences, particularly in the form of elaborate gables. Finally, Orford, once a prosperous sea port, but now cut off from the sea by Orford Ness, is dominated by its stone castle and streets of red brick cottages, many of which are built around the village green. Again, the Dutch influence abounds.

Unlike the towns and villages that have grown organically over the centuries, 20th century developments such as airbases and nuclear power stations are, for the most part, unrelated to the surrounding landscape, their designs neither reflecting local vernacular, nor making a positive contribution to the AONB. In most cases they have a significant and negative impact on the quality of the landscape. At a

Aldeburgh's colour-washed buildings face straight onto the shingle beach.

smaller scale, residential development has also generally failed to respond to the traditional use of local materials and building styles. Newer houses tend to conform to designs that may be found the length and breadth of Britain.

Halls, houses and designed landscapes

The landscape of the Suffolk Coast and Heaths derives much of its value from its wild and remote atmosphere. Nevertheless, designed landscapes are an important element in the landscape, particularly along the southern estuaries and in the northern part of the AONB. In these parts of the AONB the layout of woodlands, tree clumps, shelter-belts and parkland trees around grand houses often make a dramatic contribution to the local landscape, particularly where they are in prominent locations.

The Stour and Orwell estuaries have long been popular locations for large houses, often set in parkland. This is because of their proximity to Ipswich and connections to London, the fine views that can be gained from relatively steep estuary slopes and because of the rivers' importance for shipping and commerce. Indeed, many of the houses are associated with famous naval or maritime families.

At Holbrook on the north side of the Stour is the Royal Hospital School, built in the 1920s and 1930s for the children of officers serving in the Royal Navy. The school is an impressive set piece, set in wooded parkland running down to the river below. Just west of Shotley lies Erwarton Hall, an Elizabethan mansion which, though lacking a formal parkland landscape, is remarkable for its gateway.

The Orwell has a similar number of large houses and halls, and their parkland and grounds help to give the estuary its predominantly wooded appearance. Freston Park, on the southern side, dates back to the 16th century. It is set in what Scarfe [12] described as a "beautiful park of oaks and full grown copper beeches beside the shore of the Orwell estuary". Further east lies Woolverstone Hall, built towards the end of the 18th century, and set in an 32 ha park, enjoying wide views along the Orwell.

Erwarton's Jacobean gateway is one of the most extravagant features of the many halls and large houses found along the Orwell and Stour Rivers.

Orwell Park, sitting as it does on a promontory, is the most significant estate on the northern side of the river. The Park was laid out in 1764 by Lord Orwell, later passing to the Vernon family, the famous Admiral Vernon having been its owner at one time. Today Orwell Park retains its parkland atmosphere with single or clumps of trees on the hill slope and an area of damp oak woodland fringing the river at Nacton Shore. Orwell House now accommodates a school.

Next to Orwell Park is Broke House (originally Nacton Hall), an impressive red brick mansion set between blocks of woodland. The grounds were designed by Humphry Repton at the end of the 18th century. Broke House was the home of another famous naval figure, Sir Philip Bowes Vere Broke (1776–1841).

Bawdsey Manor, on the coast just north of the mouth of the Deben estuary was built by Sir Cuthbert Quilter in 1886. The house was set in grounds that were specially designed to withstand the battering of winds off the North Sea, with a 150 feet high rockery and a sunken garden. Bawdsey Manor, which is now empty, was occupied by the Ministry of Defence between 1936 and 1990, a use reflected by the tall radio mast that still towers over the surrounding trees.

North of Blythburgh lies Henham Park. The park was laid out in 1791 for the owner, Sir John Rous, by Humphry Repton. Today the park comprises the remains of the 85 ha pleasure grounds and about 250 ha of well-wooded parkland with several avenues and drives. Close to the northern boundary of the AONB lies Benacre Park surrounding the hall that was built in the 18th century for Thomas Carthew. The Park itself is populated with mature avenues and impressive spreading oaks.

The Benacre estate is equally impressive, providing one of the AONB's best examples of a well-managed country estate, making a positive contribution to the character of the agricultural landscape. It includes characteristic blocks of woodland, tree lined roads, maintained hedgerows and many traditional farm buildings.

Other significant estates include Staverton Park, Sudbourne Park and the area around Sutton Hall and many were associated with influential families such as the Wentworths, Gooches and Greenwells. These estates' numerous shelter-belts and coverts often make an important contribution to the landscape, since without them views over the rolling landscape would be long and wide.

Earlier sections of this report have shown how the landscape of the Suffolk Coast and Heaths has been greatly influenced by human activities. Original forest was felled to provide land for cultivation, but quickly degenerated to heathland that has since been afforested or improved to support agriculture. Similarly, centuries of drainage and flood protection have transformed many of the characteristic marshes into pasture or even arable land. In common with most parts of Britain, the pace of change has quickened during the present century, and the prospects are that the area will continue to change in the future.

In this chapter, the major prospects for future change in the AONB are examined in the context of the changes that have already taken place this century. They will be among the issues addressed by the management plan for the area, to be prepared by the Suffolk Coast and Heaths Joint Advisory Committee (JAC).

Coastal erosion and sea-level rise

Suffolk's coast and estuaries are balanced in a delicate equilibrium, but are subject to a range of pressures that have the potential to bring about significant changes. The last few decades have seen a growing awareness of the possibility of increased storminess and sea-level rise as a consequence of global warming. Some predictions suggest that sea-level will rise by up to 60 cm over the next 60 years, with serious implications for low-lying areas like the Suffolk coast.

Agencies can respond to the threat of rising sea-level in two ways. Conventional wisdom suggests that the increasing risk of flooding should be tackled by improving flood defences. In some cases such improvement will be achieved by increasing the height of the flood defence embankments that already surround areas of drained marsh and run along the banks of the estuaries and rivers. In other cases this will not be possible and more highly engineered solutions such as sheet piling may have to be employed. However these have potentially damaging effects on coastal or estuarine landscapes.

An alternative strategy, which could actually enhance the landscape rather than damage it, is to manage the retreat of flood defences, allowing areas that have been drained in the past to revert to marsh. Given the need to reduce agricultural over-production, such a policy could represent a beneficial means of withdrawing land from cultivation while at the same time creating new vistas and habitats. The AONB already has examples of defences breaking down unintentionally, eg along the Alde and Blyth estuaries, but the extent of marsh drainage in the past means that there is much potential throughout the area for planned retreat.

It is likely that rising sea-levels will reduce the width of the intertidal zone along flood defences, a phenomenon known as 'coastal squeeze'. This zone is particularly important for wildlife, supporting a range of salt tolerant plants, and forming the feeding grounds for a number of wading birds. It is also an important element in the landscape of the estuaries, the extensive areas of mudflats and saltings being essential to their character. Unless managed retreat of flood defences can be used as a means of maintaining the intertidal zone, it is likely that sea-level rise will have significant nature conservation and landscape impacts.

Mudflats such as these on the Orwell are already suffering erosion as a result of dredging to maintain a channel for commercial shipping. Rising sea-level could add further pressures to these important intertidal areas.

In estuaries like the Orwell and Stour, the intertidal areas are already under pressure. Dredging and over-deepening of the channels used by commercial shipping is believed to have increased tidal scour, threatening the stability of the mudflats. Research is required to determine the true effects of channel dredging and to establish whether material removed from the channel could be used to slow the rate of mud flat erosion.

Flood defences are also an important issue along low-lying sections of the coast. At Southwold, for instance, groynes and some of the most unsightly and intrusive types of concrete coastal protection have been used to stabilise the coast and reduce the rate of erosion. At Slaughden, the narrow neck of Orford Ness has been reinforced with large boulders and piles of shingle to prevent it from being breached by winter storms. An element of uncertainty is added by the offshore dredging of marine aggregates. Little research has been undertaken on this subject, but it is thought that such dredging may remove material that would otherwise replenish the shingle beaches, upsetting the delicate balance of coastal processes, and increasing the rate of coastal erosion. The AONB management plan should include guidelines on the visual design aspects of the construction and maintenance of flood defences with the aim of maintaining the required level of protection while minimising their impact on the landscape of the coast.

Erosion has eaten away at Suffolk's cliffs over many centuries. One potential effect of global warming is an increase in the frequency and severity of storms. Since cliff erosion is most severe during storms, an acceleration of land lost to the sea is therefore a possibility. It is important that the response to this threat takes full account of the interdependency of coastal processes and the special character of the cliff landscapes. Attempts to slow cliff erosion by the construction of defences along their base would have serious visual impacts and could prevent the replenishment of shingle beaches, thus increasing the risk of erosion and flooding elsewhere. A more effective strategy may be to accept the loss of land to the sea and to anticipate and plan for its consequences.

The National Rivers Authority has recently undertaken the Anglian Sea Defence Study in order to develop a coastal defence strategy. Management of the AONB should ensure that conservation constraints are integrated within flood defence plans, and should encourage the use of the strategy to identify areas where there is potential for the managed retreat of flood defences.

The transition from shingle beach to the marsh or drained marsh behind is one of the most important inter-relationships in the coastal landscape. The area behind the shingle beach is known as dune-slack, comprising a sloping area of shingle colonised by a range of plants that exploit the relative shelter from wind and spray. In a number of places this has suffered degradation, either with the spread of development from surrounding higher ground as at Southwold and Thorpeness, or where it has been used as a site for boat yards or car parks as at Slaughden and Dunwich. Such development is significant because it upsets the traditional character of the coastal landscape and may result in the dune-slack being regarded as little more than rough wasteland. The importance of these areas should be recognised, and policies designed that protect and enhance them.

Development

Because of its relatively isolated position, and the severance of the coast by the estuaries, the area has not experienced the same pressure for development as some other parts of Britain. There are, however, some important exceptions to this, particularly around the edges of the AONB where settlements such as Ipswich and Lowestoft place development and recreation pressure on the Orwell estuary and the Hundred River valley. Also ports such as Felixstowe and Parkeston Quay continue to expand. The area also contains a number of quasi-national interests such as nuclear power stations and redundant airbases which have particular implications for the landscape. Future improvements in the transport network may also increase the pressure for development.

Housing

Recent housing development in the AONB has been comparatively limited and the scale of development has generally been small, often taking the form of infill building or development at the edge of towns and villages. In general, such development has fairly limited impacts on the wider landscape, though the design and location of such buildings should ensure that the character of the settlement in question is not adversely affected. However, in a number of locations a few houses have been built along ridge lines adjoining settlements. For example, at Blythburgh a line of new white houses forms a south-eastward extension to the village along the side of the estuary. Although these houses undoubtedly benefit from fine views they themselves often detract from the wider landscape. The impact of building houses on the dune-slack behind shingle beaches has already been noted.

A small number of more extensive housing developments have taken place in the area, but have generally been steered to locations where impacts on more sensitive landscapes are minimised. The genteel character and charm of Southwold, for example, has been maintained by restricting growth to nearby Reydon, though even this settlement cannot accommodate much more additional growth.

There are two major concerns regarding further housebuilding in the AONB. The first is the growing difficulty that is being experienced in accommodating new growth within existing settlements. The second concern relates to the design of new buildings, and the choice of building materials. In many parts of the AONB gentle landform means that views extend over a considerable distance. Reductions in tree cover and the loss of hedgerows in particular mean that even buildings constructed along traditional lines, using Suffolk brick or pink render are visible from a long way off.

These issues can be addressed in several ways. Firstly, local planning authorities can, through their development plans, ensure that new housing development is limited to locations where its visual impact is limited. Aldeburgh serves as a good example since the most recent housing development on the flat land above the town compares favourably with that which occurred previously along the ridge to the north of the Alde. Local authorities through their plans together with non-statutory design briefs should also try to influence the design of new houses, ensuring that they blend into the landscape rather than stand out from it. Finally, where existing buildings are considered to have a major impact on the landscape, the use of appropriate screening might be considered. These policies will be all the more important since the improvement of the A12 is likely to stimulate demand for housing in the area.

A final issue relating to housing provision in the AONB is the conversion of redundant agricultural buildings to dwellings. This can be a mixed blessing; since although providing an alternative use for the building, the accompanying lawns, parked cars, horse paddocks and other domestic paraphernalia can change the character of its setting significantly. Although such changes tend to be localised, taken together they can result in an unacceptable 'domestication' of the otherwise rural and often wild and remote landscape. Further conversions should be strictly controlled.

Large-scale development

Management of the AONB should reflect the fact that some of the military structures – such as the concrete pill boxes and military research buildings at Orford Ness – are now of historic importance and should be preserved alongside the Martello Towers dating back to the Napoleonic Wars. In places such as on Orford Ness, however, there is considerable scope for tidying of the dereliction left by military activities, and the restoration of previously lost natural habitats.

There is currently great uncertainty about the future of the airforce bases at Bentwaters and Rendlesham. The US Airforce will cease operations in 1993 and the Ministry of Defence has indicated that there is unlikely to be a long-term military use for them. There is, therefore a prospect of two large redundant airbases, with their huge runways and associated housing and community facilities coming onto the market for redevelopment. The nature of such development is currently very uncertain, though it is likely that the housing and community facilities would be exploited to provide civilian accommodation. However, the scale of potential development that might arise within the AONB, together with secondary effects such as traffic generation and recreation pressures, are clearly a major cause for concern. On a more positive note, it is important that the opportunities for landscape enhancement are recognised and policies for heathland re-creation or woodland planting are incorporated into redevelopment plans. The airfields are currently divorced from the surrounding countryside and redevelopment should be used to integrate these areas fully.

Mineral extraction

Mineral extraction has also had an impact on the area, though it is often not highly visible. The building industry's growing demands for aggregates makes the sands and gravels of the sandlings an increasingly valuable resource. The area is peppered with small pits, dug over the last few centuries to extract sand, gravel, or the crag, which was found to be a valuable fertiliser. More recent gravel pits are on an altogether different scale. A number are concentrated around Wangford and immediately north of Henham Park. Although the embankments around the pits mean they are not immediately visible, in places the heaps of processed sand and gravel can be clearly seen, and are an incongruous element in this protected landscape. Tight controls should continue to be exerted over mineral workings within the AONB, and particular attention paid to the processing and storage of sand and gravel as well as their extraction. Mineral workings should not be permitted in highly visible locations.

Tall structures

Tall structures in the Suffolk Coasts and Heaths are not always at odds with the character of the landscape, as we have seen in the case of church towers and lighthouses. However, in this century the construction of radio masts, water towers, the occasional farm silo, and the pylons serving Sizewell power station, are very visible in this subtle landscape and do not necessarily enhance it. Although, as yet, no such schemes have been proposed, wind turbines would also fall into this category. Future proposals for such developments should be assessed in terms of their visibility, and their impact on the surrounding landscape.

Transport improvements

Many people attribute the special atmosphere of the Suffolk Coast and Heaths to its relatively isolated position, and the difficulty encountered in moving up or down the coast. The proposed upgrading of the A12 to a dual carriageway however will mean that the area is increasingly accessible for visitors and commuters alike, generating pressure for further development and possibly leading to the commercialisation of towns like Aldeburgh and Southwold. It is important that local authorities and other agencies in the AONB should be prepared for the increased pressure for development, and the growth in visitor numbers that may follow these road improvements. The development pressures associated with recreation are discussed below.

A new dual carriageway road could have significant landscape impacts where it crosses the Blyth valley (the existing A12 runs through Blythburgh), and the lower part of the Hundred River valley. These are vulnerable landscapes, and agencies should negotiate to ensure that the least damaging road alignments and designs are selected and that the maximum amount of environmental protection and improvement is incorporated as part of the schemes.

Light pollution

Light pollution is a growing problem in the AONB. For the most part at night the countryside is shrouded in darkness, reflecting its undeveloped character. However, a series of recent developments stand out, brightly lit or casting an orange glow onto the dark sky, highly visible over a considerable distance. These include the radio masts on Orford Ness; the airbases; Sizewell power station; docks at Felixstowe and Parkeston and junctions of the A12. It is likely that the proposed improvement of the A12 will include increased levels of street lighting. This light pollution has a serious impact on the night landscape of the AONB, undermining its remote and unspoilt character. Both lighting levels and methods used should be very carefully assessed in order to prevent or limit pollution. Only essential lighting should be permitted.

Agriculture

Farming has traditionally been one of the main agents for change in the landscape of the Suffolk Coast and Heaths. In this century the trends of agricultural reclamation of heathland and marshes have continued and have resulted in the intensification of agriculture and marked changes in the landscape. In the process, traditional landscape elements have been lost and the structure of the landscape eroded.

Although many of these trends continue to impact on the landscape of the AONB, in recent years a number of factors have together resulted in a move back towards more environmentally sensitive farming

The loss of hedgerows in the sandlings, such as here near Easton Broad, creates open landscapes where the Suffolk sky is often the most dramatic feature.

practices, and the reversal of some of these adverse changes. The CAP has led to over production in some sectors and reviews have led to a series of measures designed to reduce levels of such surpluses. Farmers have been encouraged to set-aside land by payment of incentives and the most recent reforms have introduced a new arable regime that requires arable farmers to compulsorily set-aside 15 per cent of their arable land on a rotational basis. Set-aside fields are often quite visible in the AONB landscape because of the contrast they make with adjoining cultivated arable fields. Since set-aside is usually temporary, farmers are not generally encouraged to accept landscape or conservation measures on this land, so there are few long-term benefits for the landscape. Land in the AONB that has been set-aside under the previous 5-year scheme has been eligible for the Countryside Commission's Countryside Premium scheme, which aims to create positive environmental improvements such as wildlife fallow areas, meadowland with public access, or wooded margins around fields. A few areas have joined this scheme.

Apart from a recognition that there is no longer a need for ever increasing production, there has also been growing pressure to reverse the damaging effects of agricultural intensification on the environment. At the same time the need to maintain farmer's income has been recognised and as a result a number of schemes have been established to provide financial incentives for environmentally sensitive farming.

In the AONB a number of the coastal marshes, estuaries and river valleys, along the Rivers Ore, Alde, Upper Blyth, Deben, Minsmere and Hundred, have been included within the MAFF's Suffolk River Valleys Environmentally Sensitive Area (ESA). In this area farmers are paid incentives to retain and manage traditional permanent grassland, or to allow arable land to revert to grassland. In the whole of the ESA, including part of the Dedham Vale AONB, 76 per cent of eligible land has been entered into the scheme, representing something like 25 per cent of the land in each of the valleys. Most land has been restored to traditional management, with more modest, though still substantial, areas of arable land being allowed to revert. This is a major scheme that has had a significant impact in conserving and enhancing the landscape and reverting the trends that, over the years, have led to loss of the distinctive river valley landscapes.

The Countryside Stewardship scheme introduced in 1991 by the Countryside Commission has much in common with the ESA scheme, in that it provides incentives for farmers to manage land in environmentally beneficial ways or to re-create traditional landscape features from cultivated land. In the Suffolk Coast and Heaths, payments are available for coastal landscapes; riverside landscapes and lowland heath and there is considerable interest in the scheme in areas that are not covered by the ESA. Countryside Stewardship has been particularly important in respect of the management and restoration of heaths.

These schemes have begun to reverse the long process of agricultural intensification and hold out the prospect of retaining and restoring some of the traditional character of the AONB landscape. The prospects are perhaps best in the river valleys, estuaries and coastal areas, where the incentives, combined in some places with the withdrawal of sea defences, provide the mechanism to re-create the traditional pattern of these landscapes. The need is to encourage the widest possible up-take of the incentives, and to try to target management and restoration to achieve the greatest possible effect, perhaps by encouraging groups of adjoining landowners to work together.

Trees and woodland

The three major coniferous forests established by the Forestry Commission at Rendlesham, Tunstall and Dunwich were, by the 1980s, reaching maturity. However, the 1987 storm caused severe damage both to these forests and to many of the shelter-belts and other woods throughout the area. The Forestry Commission quickly instituted a programme of clearing the fallen trees and replanting. However, the landscape of the three forests is still a damaged and desolate one, with piles of fallen trees interspersed between areas of new planting, and the sometimes ragged remnants of the old forest left standing in occasional blocks or lines.

The Forestry Commission has taken the opportunity presented by the storm to begin increasing the nature conservation and recreation interest of the new forests

The 1987 storm caused severe damage to forests in the area.

by changes in layout, structure and the types of trees planted. The replanted forests will include a higher proportion of open space, both along ridges and tracks, and in the form of clearings. It is hoped that heather, which grew here before afforestation, will regenerate in these areas. The clearings will also provide valuable habitats for woodlarks and other woodland birds and animals. The Phoenix Trail, developed in Rendlesham Forest, is an example of the new emphasis on recreation. The mature forests that were largely destroyed by the 1987 storm were being managed to create a diverse age structure, with different areas being felled each year. This was giving the woodland a varied appearance, with blocks of mature trees juxtaposed with young or middle-aged trees. The devastation of such large areas, and the commercial pressures to replant the 'crop' of conifers means that the opportunity to create a heterogeneous woodland structure has been reduced. However, the Forestry Commission's replanting designs include 'scalloped' woodland edges and it is hoped that these, with broader rides and margins along roads, will reduce the landscape impact of dense areas of conifers.

It is apparent that many tress in the AONB are dead or dying. This is attributed to a variety of factors. Dutch elm disease has been particularly severe in Suffolk where a high proportion of hedgerow trees were elms. The disease arrived comparatively late in the area and many dead elms still stand along field boundaries and the sides of country lanes. In other cases, the damage was caused by the 1987 storm. Elsewhere, coastal retreat has exposed trees to increased levels of salt spray and falling groundwater levels. There is more speculation about other causes of tree damage. It may be that the combination of a number of dry summers and increases in groundwater abstraction for irrigation have had the effect of lowering the watertable in some areas, depriving trees of their source of water. Acid rain, generated by industrial areas further west may also be a contributory factor. Whatever the causes, the loss of so many trees is a cause for concern, particularly given the already significant losses associated with agricultural improvements described earlier.

Management of the AONB should tackle the problems of tree damage and loss in two ways. First, research should be undertaken to determine the causes of tree losses so that further damage can be reduced or more tolerant species introduced. Second, and equally important, the key opportunities for replanting trees should be identified. The priorities should include:

- dead, dying or lost trees along lanes and in hedges, copses and shelter-belts;

- damaged and 'gappy' hedgerows and shelter-belts in the sandlings and on estuary and river valley slopes;

- structural woodland such as the line of trees that should mark the break of slope between marsh and hill slope;

- hedgerows, copses and shelter-belts that have been entirely lost, but whose location can be identified from old maps and aerial photographs.

Heathland

Heathland is now regarded as a valued resource, not only locally but also at a national level. Within the AONB, a range of organisations positively promote the management and re-creation of heathland in areas where it was previously lost. The Sandlings Group, for instance, is an informal coalition of conservation bodies and local authorities that aims to conserve and enhance the remaining areas of heath. The RSPB have initiated an ambitious project to re-create heathland on land previously reclaimed for agriculture. They have purchased arable land neighbouring their Minsmere reserve and plan gradually to reduce the soil's fertility and re-establish heathland plant communities, thereby increasing the range of habitats for birds in the area. Elsewhere, particularly on smaller areas of heath such as at Snape Warren and Blaxhall Heath, birch and pine have invaded the heath, signalling the beginning of its degeneration to scrub. The grazing of sheep can be an effective and traditional method of management that can help suppress the invasion of heath by other species. Suffolk Wildlife Trust have already re-introduced flocks of sheep onto Sutton Common, and plan to do so elsewhere, provided that issues of fencing to contain the stock can be resolved.

Recreation

The tranquillity of Suffolk Coast and Heaths landscape means that recreational pressures are an important issue. The attractive character of the coastal towns and the difficulty in moving north and south along the coast means that visitors tend to be concentrated in centres such as Aldeburgh, Southwold or Dunwich. This concentration generally means that the effects of tourism can be contained and managed, with relatively few pressures on areas that are more sensitive in terms of nature conservation or landscape.

However, there are a number of exceptions to this, and the pressures brought by recreation are increasing throughout the area. Growing numbers of people are visiting the area, attracted both by its special character and by its rare wildlife. Recreation is generally informal, and a greater number of walkers and bird watchers now penetrate relatively remote areas, increasing pressure for footpath improvement, signing and car parking provision. Increasing litter is another unwelcome result. The large number of nature conservation areas such as those at Minsmere, Boyton Marshes and Trimley Marshes is having a similar effect, and they often incorporate car parks, visitor centres, boardwalks and hides. Though individually these have a fairly limited impact, taken as a whole there is a danger that they will undermine the qualities that attract people in the first place. The AONB management plan must develop a recreation strategy that addresses the landscape impacts associated with increased visitor numbers. The plan should provide guidelines on the design and location of car parks, visitor centres, hides, footpaths and signing. Each such development should be assessed in terms of its impact on the landscape.

The coast and estuaries are becoming increasingly attractive as a place for water-skiing and jet-skiing. These forms of recreation conflict with the serene atmosphere of the estuaries, and disrupt the peace, both by their persistent noise and by their frenetic

The area is attracting growing numbers of visitors.

activity. These activities should be carefully controlled and monitored, and should be steered to areas where impacts on the atmosphere of the area are minimised.

Boating has an impact too. Although yachts are an accepted and, some would say, attractive element in the landscape of the estuaries, many stretches of water are close to their capacity. Many people feel that further increases in numbers of boats, and of the jetties and huts that serve them, would undermine the character of the estuaries' gentle landscape. The type of moorings is also important. As already noted, in specific places such as Pin Mill and Waldringfield, clusters of boats along the rivers are now regarded as a traditional part of the landscape. Marinas, however, with their concentration of masts, their sheds and cranes, and the areas given over to car parking and storage have a much more significant impact on the estuarine landscape, particularly during the winter months when many boats are stored out of the water. In places like Martlesham Creek, the growing demand for additional moorings is reflected in the incremental and uncoordinated growth of jetties and moorings, effectively creating small marinas.

Pressure to permit new marina development within the AONB or to expand moorings into quiet and secluded parts of the estuaries should be resisted. There should also be a limit placed on the number of boats using the estuaries. The special character of moorings and jetties at places such as Southwold Harbour and Pin Mill should be protected.

Even where recreation is well contained and managed, there are sometimes concerns about facilities such as car parks, which are often difficult to site without encroaching on this open landscape. At Dunwich, an area of car parking has been created on the dune-slack behind the beach, while at the nearby National Trust property of Dunwich Heath, car parking crowns the hill overlooking Minsmere nature reserve. Relocation or screening may be appropriate ways of reducing these impacts. The small car park to the west of Walberswick is a good example, sited below the surrounding ground level in a former gravel pit.

The shingle beaches along the Suffolk coast are a sensitive natural habitat as well as being an important landscape feature. However, Orford Ness, long the haunt of bird watchers and fishermen, is coming under new pressure from visitors who use four-wheel-drive and all-terrain vehicles to gain access. Such use has the potential to upset the delicate balance of landscape and ecology and should be prohibited.

In common with many other parts of Britain, the Suffolk Coast and Heaths have recently come under increasing pressure for golf course development. To date, such developments have been limited to sites on the sandlings, for instance at Aldeburgh and, away from the estuaries and coast where they could be visible from a considerable distance. Golf courses should continue to be resisted in these more sensitive locations. However, with reductions in agricultural production and parallel pressures for farm diversification, it is possible that in the sandlings, the development of sensitively designed golf courses could represent a means of re-creating heathland landscapes in areas that were previously reclaimed for agriculture. Other forms of farm diversification should also be considered, and the AONB management plan should suggest alternatives such as nature reserves that are in keeping with the character of the landscape and that could help reduce visitor pressures elsewhere.

Marinas can have a significant impact on the estuarine landscape.

A landscape can assume national significance not only because of its particular character and qualities, but also because of special cultural associations that it may have with nationally important characters, writers and artists. Examination of the way that others have perceived the landscape over time can also provide pointers to a consensus view on why an area is considered special, and what particular features have consistently attracted attention and comment. Both these perspectives on the perceptions of the landscape of the Suffolk Coast and Heaths are reviewed below.

Literary and musical connections

Perhaps the Suffolk coast's most famous writer was the poet George Crabbe. He was born in Aldeburgh in 1754 and wrote a series of poems such as 'The Village' and 'The Borough' in which he tried to describe the realities of rural life. In the words of Tennyson [13],

> "It was the beauty of Suffolk that he set himself to give to the world – the beauty of fields, trees, rivers and valleys. Often he saw it as a frowning, brooding beauty, yet always he infused it with that freshness and delight which, in his eyes, shone upon every leaf and every cloud. Landscape was his life and joy, and landscape he perfected."

One of the most famous writers to have lived in the area was Edward Fitzgerald, translator of the *Rubaiyat of Omar Khayyam*. Tennyson [13] describes how Fitzgerald 'gave himself up to the river Deben even more devotedly than did John Constable to the river Stour'. Fitzgerald lived near Woodbridge and spent much of his time sailing his boat *The Scandal* around the coast and along the estuaries.

Another writer who gained inspiration from the water was Arthur Ransome who lived for a time at Broke Hall Farm on the Orwell opposite Pin Mill. Several of his children's books including *We Didn't Mean to go to Sea* were set in and around the Orwell.

The composer Benjamin Britten is often associated with the landscape of the Suffolk Coast and Heaths. He was born in Lowestoft and grew up around Aldeburgh. It was when he was living in the windmill at Snape that he wrote *Peter Grimes*, an opera based on Crabbe's poem 'The Borough'. Soon after, he moved to Aldeburgh, and with Peter Pears founded the Aldeburgh Festival. In the 1960s buildings at Snape Maltings were converted into a concert hall to accommodate the festival. Since 1979 the extensive maltings complex has also housed the Britten-Pears School for Advanced Musical Studies.

Scarfe [12] described the setting of the Maltings: "near the wind rustled reeds of the river, a place of exultation, and exaltation, for the musical and the expressive from all over the world".

Artists and the landscape

The Suffolk Coast and Heaths became popular among contemporary artists in the middle of the 19th century, reflecting the changing fashions in landscape painting. Turner's paintings of Dunwich, Orford Ness and Aldeburgh are early examples of the attractiveness of the area to artists. In the second half of the 19th century British artists followed the French trend of depicting harsh rural life. In Britain this focused on the fisherman, and coastal scenes became increasingly important.

Walberswick quickly developed as a centre for artists, especially after *The Pier Head, Walberswick* was painted by Philip Wilson Steer in 1888. Other examples from this period include W J Steggles' *The Quay at Walberswick* and Walter Osborne's *An October Morning*. Charles Keene and Charles Rennie Mackintosh were also notable visitors. Mackintosh painted a series of watercolours of local plants, together with scenes at Walberswick and along the Blyth. Edward Seago also painted Blythburgh. Aldeburgh also attracted artists and notable works include Claude Rogers' *Figures on an Aldeburgh Beach* and Ethelbert White's *Boats at Aldeburgh*.

By the mid-20th century, east Suffolk was increasingly appreciated for the combination of coastal scenes, marsh, heath and of course its estuaries. The combination of heathland and pines with coast appears in many pictures. Writing about art and the countryside, Pennington [14] regarded the Suffolk

Coast and Heaths as being a distinctive area within East Anglia, describing the

> "lonely, bleak and sometimes colourful coast where the rivers Alde, Deben and Orwell come down to the sea ... a coastline that varies between low cliffs and sand or shingle beaches, with heathland rising above the estuaries and a feeling of remoteness which more than compensates for its lack of spectacular scenes".

The photographer Edwin Smith was much attracted to the area. His moody photographs of Minsmere and the Blyth illustrate the text of James Turner's *The Countryside of Britain* [15].

Descriptive writings

A number of descriptive writings focus on the landscape of the Suffolk Coast and Heaths. While earlier descriptions concentrated on the need to improve the agriculture of the area by reclaiming heath and draining marsh, more recent writers have focused on the beauty and subtle charm of the Suffolk Coast and Heaths. Many of the writers, including Tennyson, Blyth and Scarfe have lived and breathed the landscape for all or part of their lives, and their very personal accounts capture the intimate and subtle qualities of this landscape. A common thread running through most of the recent descriptions is a concern with change and the forces that could change the landscape.

In 1735, John Kirby wrote *The Suffolk Traveller* [16], noting three main types of landscape in the county as a whole and dividing the coastal sandlands (or sandlings) into marsh, agriculture and heathland. Tennyson [13], writing in the 1930s, observed that "On the Suffolk coast there is every type of land known in England, all jumbled together and fitting into a quite irregular pattern". Arnott [10] describes the variety and change associated with the Suffolk Coast and Heaths:

> "I love equally the waterways and the countryside through which they run. When you are on the rivers, you feel remote from the life of the land, and when you are ashore, the salt water seems far away. This sudden change is one of the charms of sailing, for here on the East Coast, land and sea are delightfully mingled."

Dymond [17] emphasises the subtlety of the Suffolk landscape, noting that panoramas are rare and the scene constantly changing as one travels through it.

Several writers have highlighted the particular physical conditions that occur along the Suffolk coast. In 1771, Arthur Young [18] noted the fact that along the coast "There is a large amount of poor and even blowing sand to be found ... The whole of the maritime region may be termed sandy". He went on to describe the climate of the Suffolk coast as being "Unquestionably one of the dryest climates in the kingdom. The frosts are severe and the north east winds sharp and prevalent". Hammond Innes [8] described the climate's dry harshness, noting the special quality of the Suffolk sky:

> "The artists love it, that glorious light. It is the same light, of course, that inspired Vermeer and Rembrandt and all the other great Dutch painters who had the advantage of similar brightness and breadth of skies on the other side of the North Sea."

Other writers have described the buildings and vernacular of the Suffolk Coast and Heaths. Blyth [19] highlights the extraordinary variety of materials that have been used to create Suffolk's villages, describing the oak beams and Suffolk pink, the use of flint in cottage walls and in the flushwork of church exteriors, and the use of sarsens, old stones brought to the area by ice sheets, in church towers and some of the older houses. Fitch [20] cites the prominence of churches in the Suffolk landscape:

> "And if, further, on a favourable tide, you felt disposed to sail in turn up the Stour, Orwell, Deben, Alde and Blyth, you would be rewarded with some of Suffolk's most enchanting prospects – Erwarton Church surveying the lower reaches of the Stour, Ramsholt the Deben, Iken on its promontory up the Alde and, most splendid of all, Blythburgh riding majestically at anchor overlooking the Blyth valley..."

A number of writers have concentrated on particular aspects of the landscape and the following sections illustrate how the AONB has been described over the years.

Coast

The coast is regarded by many as one of Suffolk's hidden splendours, often difficult to reach and always understated in its drama. Tennyson's [13] description of the Suffolk coastline captures its unique character. He pointed to the difficulty of actually getting to the coast, arguing that in many cases a visitor put down just one mile from the sea would find it almost impossible to reach it because of the twisting network of tracks and lanes, and the obstacles formed by marshes and rivers. However, once there, he was confident that the visitor would fall for the coastal landscape. He wrote:

> "The real glory of Suffolk is the coast, and yet it is a stretch not in the least representative of the

popular idea of England's coast-line. So much the better, for on its very difference rests its whole character and reputation."

He expresses surprise that, given the English love of dramatic cliffs, the Suffolk coast is held in such high esteem. Tennyson suggests that many visitors to Suffolk are probably unaware that there are any cliffs, but that 'for one who knows them from the seaward side their beauty is enhanced by the eternal flatness from which they rise and which makes them seem grander and more massive than they really are.'

Crabbe, in The Borough [21], wrote about the Suffolk coast on a stormy day, his description accurately reflecting the unceasing power of the sea:

"All where the eye delights, yet dreads to roam,
The breaking billows cast the flying foam
Upon the billows rising – all the deep
Is restless change; the waves so swell'd and steep,
Breaking and sinking , and the sunken swells,
Nor one lone moment, in its station dwells:"

Tennyson [13] also describes the changing moods of the sea:

"Could you see it in summer, drawling up the beach, brushing the shingle with its coquettish lips, so gentle, so harmless, so indolent, you would scoff at the idea of evil lurking in that serene and imperturbable bosom. But come to it in winter, when the same innocent sluggard is grey and cold, when the great white waves come driving in to crash and snarl against the shore, when the fishermen stand helpless on the beach beside their little boats and the wildfowl chatter uneasily in the safety of the rivers and marshes – come back to Suffolk then, and see how dreadful is the change from meekness to ferocity."

Sandling and heath

Crabbe [21] described the heaths around Aldeburgh in the 18th century, in terms of their weedy, unproductive vegetation, writing about the landscape's 'sad splendour'. Thirty years later, however, he described the surrounding heath in more glowing and appreciative terms, painting a picture that contrasted with his earlier impressions and the views of Young and other progressive agriculturalists, writing:

"Stray over the Heath in all its purple bloom-
And pick the Blossom where the wild-bees hum;
And through the broomy Bound with ease they pass
And press the sandy Sheep-walk's slender grass
Where dwarfish flowers among the gorse are spread
And the Lamb browzes by the Linnet's bed."

More recent descriptions focus on the special character of the remaining areas of heath. Tennyson [13] described the character of the heath, noting the transformations that accompany the changing seasons:

"A heath, to my mind is never dull; it is the land of eternal change. Under the grey skies of winter it is wild and forlorn, exciting and slightly antagonistic; in spring and summer it is a warm, welcoming landscape of ever-deepening colours, brown, yellow, purple and green. And the scents of the heath are scarcely the same for more than two weeks on end; what a difference, for instance, between the fresh smell of vigorous green bracken in early summer and the thick, musty odour that seems to press up from the damp earth on a bleak mid-winter's afternoon."

Lee Chadwick [4], a local writer who has spent much of her life living on the heath, learning about its history and observing its life describes the nocturnal qualities of the heath:

"...when at night under the huge globe of sky, the dark clumps of gorse and weird shapes of tangled briar crouch like sleeping beasts as the moon climbs out of the sea, the stillness seems to stretch back to the very beginnings of time..."

Other writers have described the forests that now cover parts of the sandlings, showing the varied opinions that they provoke. Arnott [5], writing about Rendlesham and Tunstall Forests, argued that such large plantations were out of place in the landscape of the Suffolk sandlings:

"The neat orderly rows of fir trees growing ever darker and more dismal, do not accord with the Suffolk scene of open heath and lush, green swale. Far rather would I have seen the flocks of Suffolk sheep restored to these wide lands where they used to be."

Hammond Innes [8], on the other hand, was fond of these forests, comparing them favourably with those of nearby Breckland:

"Perhaps I am prejudiced, having watched them develop from quite small trees, but I prefer these coastal forests to Breckland, the plantations more broken, patches of farmland and always the flickering yellow of kissing-time gorse merging in summer with the brighter brilliance of broom. A great place for fungi in the gold of autumn, a world removed that puts one in the mood on the way to Snape and the Aldeburgh Festival..."

Estuaries

The estuaries along the Suffolk coast have long been associated with shipping and sailing, providing sites for sheltered ports like Ipswich and Woodbridge, and more recently havens for yachts and other pleasure craft.

Many of the writings about the estuaries reflect these associations, but also highlight the tranquil atmosphere that pervades these tidal rivers.

Michael Drayton's epic poem the 'Polyolbion' [22], written in 1622, described the "Suffolcean floods", noting how each river flowed east to the coast rather than south to join the Stour, referring to the Ore as "a flood of wondrous fame", and the Blyth, "a dainty brook".

Crabbe [21] also wrote about the marshy estuaries in 'The Borough', his tale about Peter Grimes, later immortalised in Benjamin Britten's opera:

"When tides were neap, and, in the sultry day,
Through the tall bounding mud-banks made their
    way,
Which on each side rose swelling, and below
The dark warm flood ran silently and slow;
There anchoring, Peter chose from man to hide,
There hang his head, and view the lazy tide
In its hot slimy channel slowly glide."

At the turn of the century, George Gissing [11] described the tranquillity of the Blyth estuary, its water, its meadows and the heath along its slopes. Tennyson [13] spent his formative years exploring the Alde estuary. He described the view from Iken, highlighting the huge expanse of water that is the river below and describing the scene at low tide when "you will see the whole river fall away until it becomes a flat, shining ocean of mud with the channel a thin thread through the middle of it".

Francis Engleheart [23] graphically described the scene at Pin Mill on the Orwell:

"But the eye wanders as the sunshafts lower.
Here is a wash of oyster-coloured ooze
Tongued with the turquoise thrusting of the flood,
The insinuating seas that, twisting wry
In a Suffolk tideway, spill their strength and lose
The aspiring water welling in a sigh.
Here is the press of an insistent blood,
The pulse of power.

It vivifies; it fills. Here in the bay
The leaning masts, awakening, ride upright.
As jewels move upon a breathing breast
So gentle sway the little coloured craft
On this resurgent bosom. Lifting light
They swing to the stream. Landward a voice has
    laughed
Out of the huddle of homes that proffer rest
At the close of the day."

The artist Edward Seago [24] described the appearance of yachts on the estuaries:

Pin Mill *by Edward Seago. (Reproduced with kind permission of the Edward Seago Estate.)*

"With the first fresh winds of summer the river yachts leave their winter moorings – their white sails appear all over the marshes like butterflies in sunshine. All summer long there is scarcely a day when those scattered flecks of white are absent from the landscape."

Hammond Innes' recent description [8] epitomises the tranquil beauty that is so much a part of the estuaries' landscape:

"Early in the morning, and in the evening, that is when the estuaries are at their best – the stillness and the brightness, the gentle murmur of the current as the tide makes or falls, light slanting on the water, the banks mirrored in its surface, the silver of a fish jumping, ripples widening on a circle. But more than anything else, I think, it is those wide uninterrupted skies, so sparklingly clear and blue in the morning, the cloud galleons forming as the sun warms the land and then at evening the skies clearing again. And the curlews, always the curlews."

Marshes and river valleys

Until this century, it appears that the marshes were regarded as waste, a resource that should be drained to provide pasture for cattle. Today the remaining areas of marsh are highly valued because of their contribution to the landscape and their nature conservation value. Tennyson [13], writing about marshes on the Alde, painted an evocative picture that captures the attraction of the reed beds and saltings:

"The marsh has a character and an atmosphere, a mystery and a rarity that cannot be transcribed. Certainly a great deal of its outward charm comes from contrast with its setting... But it is the nature of the marsh that enthrals you, its loneliness, its wildness, its freedom, its peculiar flowers and birds and animals."

In 1923, Dutt [25] wrote about the rich wildlife of the marshes, describing the range of birds that feed and nest in the reed beds. He wrote of the strange bleating call of the snipe, the moorhens and coots building their nests from sedge, and the calls of reed and sedge warblers that inhabit the reeds. Again, the image is one of serenity and harmony, a theme that emerges over and over again in writings about this area.

Forces for change

Appreciation of the Suffolk Coast and Heaths landscape has long been accompanied by concerns that modern progress will undermine its special qualities. Edward Fitzgerald [26], writing in the 1860s, complained that:

"The Country about here is the Cemetery of so many of my oldest Friends: and the petty race of Squires who have succeeded, only use the Earth for an Investment: cut down every old tree: level every Violet Bank: and make the old Country of my Youth hideous to me in my decline."

Arnott [5] lamented the changes that have affected the estuaries, arguing that:

"The days of quiet security and peace seem to be no more although the age-long ways and traditions linger on in the countryside and upon the coastal waters. The gaff rig with its tanned mainsail survives for a little longer but the Orford galleys and Aldeburgh cod-smacks have gone."

However, he does note that the "sails of old-time yachts and their modern counterparts still glide through the cornfields of Eastern England".

Blyth [19] describes some of the changes which have occurred during the 20th century. He argues that pre-war Suffolk was "ecologically glorious and economically stagnant. Towering hedges were full of the descendants of the oaks which had provided the timber for the houses. Immense Elms stood everywhere – coffin wood. The pastures in the river valleys during June rose to the cows' flanks. Cottages were mostly patched, rarely restored and their gardens unsophisticated and often very beautiful". Blyth wistfully refers to this as a waiting scene, "waiting for a finished Suffolk to depart, waiting for the war, waiting for the post-war transformation".

A final, more hopeful note is sounded by Tennyson [13], who argues that the very nature of the landscape is its salvation. He suggests that the "intractable marshes, the contortions of the rivers and the impossible lay-out of the country" have discouraged the "insidious" hand of man, ensuring that the rewards of developing these areas are in many cases not worth the trouble. He concluded that:

"It is supremely and unassailably isolated. The wildness of it is a most attractive hostility, which is not only its greatest charm, but its surest salvation as well. With this it has frightened off all sorts of undesirable possibilities. They will never be more than possibilities, and I shall always be able to look upon Suffolk as my own."

The importance attached to the landscape of the Suffolk Coast and Heaths is reflected in its designation in 1969 as an AONB. This indicates the significance of the landscape in national as well as regional or local terms, placing it alongside the 38 other AONBs, which together with the National Parks, represent the most prized parts of our national landscape resource.

It is now over 20 years since the Suffolk Coast and Heaths were formally designated an AONB, although as has been indicated, appreciation of this special landscape goes back several centuries. Chapter 3 outlined a range of pressures that are challenging the quality of the landscape in this area, and it is an opportune time to re-consider why it deserves the protection and management that go along with AONB designation.

Outstanding qualities

To be designated as an AONB, a landscape must have a range of unusual, unique or outstanding qualities. These may be considered under four main headings:

- the value of the landscape as part of the national landscape resource, including rarity, representativeness and comparisons with other areas of similar character;

- the scenic qualities of the landscape, including the particular combination of landscape elements, aesthetic qualities and its particular 'sense of place';

- evidence about the way the landscape is perceived and valued by the general public and by those with a particular interest in landscape;

- other values attached to the landscape, including historical and cultural associations, and special interests such as wildlife, archaeological and historical features.

The extent to which the Suffolk Coast and Heaths demonstrate these different qualities is outlined below.

A national landscape resource

One of the most important distinguishing qualities of the Suffolk Coast and Heaths is its unique combination of landscape types; it is a mosaic of heath, forest, farmland, estuaries, marshes and coast. Other AONBs have some of these elements, for example the salt-marshes and mudflats of Chichester Harbour and the coastal marshes found along the North Norfolk Coast. Nowhere else, however, does one experience the same variety of landscapes or such rapid transitions from one to another. Equally unusual is the series of estuaries that structure the landscape, dividing it into a series of geographically separate areas.

The importance of the landscape as a whole is mirrored in the significance of individual elements within it. Lowland heath, for instance, is now a nationally scarce landscape and wildlife resource and is generally protected where it still remains. Similarly, the sculpting of Suffolk's shingle beaches has produced spits and bars that are of geomorphological interest and that give the coast a unique character.

When compared with other coastal landscapes, particularly those that lie close to London, the apparent wildness and remoteness of the Suffolk Coast and Heaths is remarkable. This is partly a consequence of historically poor connections with the capital, but also reflects the fragmented character of the landscape, its division by estuaries and the problems that this poses for movement along the coast.

Scenic qualities

Much of the character and quality of the AONB landscape can be attributed to the great diversity and the combinations of individual elements. Nevertheless, the landscape of the Suffolk Coast and Heaths has a strong overall character. This is based on the marriage of the coastal landscape of cliffs, estuaries, marshes and meres, with the contrasting inland landscapes that are subtle in landform and vary from the forests, heaths and farmland of the sandlings to the often hidden river valleys. The landscape also offers a number of important contrasts at a smaller scale, for instance between the exposed shingle coast and the shelter of the estuaries, and between the natural character of the

Much of the character and quality of the AONB is due to the marriage of coastal and inland landscapes.

heathland and the intensively managed character of the farmland around it.

The coast and the estuaries are characterised by long views over the sea, mudflats, rivers or marshes. Elsewhere such extensive views are rare within the AONB. This is the result of the understated, rolling character of the landscape, and the regular blocks of wood that help to give structure to the landscape of the sandlings. As a result, the immediate landscape is constantly changing as one moves from one gentle valley to the next, or from heath into woodland, along the coast or into an estuary valley. Tall buildings often act as important reference points in this subtle and complex landscape.

A number of individual features are particularly characteristic of the Suffolk Coast and Heaths landscape. Their varying extents and the combinations in which they occur create variations in the character of the landscape and contribute to its notably diverse and complex nature.

The **coast**, with its exposed, shifting shingle beaches, and its crumbling sandy cliffs is an important and largely unspoilt part of the Suffolk landscape. The uncommercialised, rather genteel character of the coastal towns, and the sometimes ramshackle nature of the harbours, contribute positively to the quality and atmosphere of the area as a whole.

The **estuaries**, with their great variety of character and scale make an important contribution to the quality of the landscape. They range from the impressive valleys of the Stour and Orwell estuaries, with their commercial shipping and yachting to the Alde and Blyth, which are broad shallow valleys, remarkable for their peace and tranquillity. Mudflats, saltings and drained marsh shape the character of these waterways, together with the scatter of villages acting as a focus for the yachts and other pleasurecraft that abound. Added to the estuaries are the **coastal marshes**, separated from the sea by shingle beaches and often fringed by woodland inland.

The **sandlings** form a hinterland to the coast and estuaries throughout the area. Their character contributes much to the diverse nature of the landscape as a whole. Much of the sandlings area is now farmed and the drive to increase agricultural production during past decades has resulted in the amalgamation of fields and the loss of many hedgerows. However, the sandlings retain substantial areas of woodland, often in the form of shelter-belts, which give structure to this agricultural landscape, preventing the creation of the prairie-like landscapes found elsewhere in East Anglia. Scattered throughout the sandlings are the remnants of once extensive areas of lowland heath. These apparently wild areas provide a valuable foil to the regimented agricultural landscape,

as well as being an important landscape in their own right, of considerable value for both nature conservation and recreation.

Perceptions and preferences

There is no survey information available to tell us what the general public think about the landscape of the Suffolk Coast and Heaths. However, it is probably true to say that, unlike coasts with fine beaches and commercialised seaside towns, the area attracts those who prefer a more remote and wild area, and less formal activities such as rambling, boating, birdwatching or sea-fishing. More traditional, beach oriented holidays tend to be quite tightly focused in towns such as Southwold and Aldeburgh and at Felixstowe and Lowestoft on the periphery of the AONB.

A more informed, if less representative indication of people's perceptions of this landscape is provided by the work of writers and painters. Recurrent themes are the wild, exposed nature of the coast, the peaceful and natural character of the estuaries with their mudflats and boats, the mystery and ecological importance of the marshes and the wild beauty of the areas of heathland. A common concern, expressed many times over the last century, is the threat of changes that could undermine these and other special qualities of the landscape.

Other special values

The Suffolk Coast and Heaths are of great significance for nature conservation. The shingle beaches along the coast support rare and fragile plant communities and provide relatively undisturbed breeding grounds for sea birds; the mudflats, saltings and marshes of the river estuaries provide valuable habitats for plants, invertebrates and birds; and the areas of lowland heath represent an important, and nationally scarce habitat. The importance of many of these habitats is reflected in their high degree of protection demonstrated by the extent of National Nature Reserves, SSSIs and County Wildlife Sites. Organisations such as the Suffolk Wildlife Trust and the RSPB are active in the area, often acquiring land and managing it for the benefit of wildlife.

The landscape of the Suffolk Coast and Heaths is also of great archaeological and historic importance. The area is speckled with tumuli, many of which have yet to be investigated, and may reveal finds such as the outstandingly important boat-graves of Sutton Hoo and Snape. The wider landscape also retains many ancient features, with the sites of historic settlements at Iken on the Alde and Burrow Hill on the Butley

River, for instance. The field and settlement patterns reflect the process of enclosure which began in the Middle Ages, and research has indicated that the sites of many churches in the area pre-date the *Domesday book*.

Finally, the value of the landscape is underlined by historic and cultural associations, as described in Chapter 4.

Prospects for change

Many of Suffolk's older buildings reflect centuries of gradual change, the tendency being to repair and adapt rather than replace. Pantiles replaced thatch, grand brick chimneys were added to larger houses, and in some places brick, flint and stone replaced timber and plaster. In many ways, the landscape of the Suffolk Coast and Heaths has undergone a similar process of gradual, though accelerating change. The remaining areas of heathland, for example, are the product of prehistoric forest clearance and many of the field and settlement patterns date back to the Middle Ages. The buildings of coastal towns such as Orford and Aldeburgh also reflect centuries of change.

Part of the charm of the Suffolk Coast and Heaths AONB is its unhurried pace of life and its uncommercialised character, which combine to create an atmosphere, which at times, seems to be decades behind the rest of the country. This is not to deny that the area has been affected by change. One only needs to visit Sizewell, or to watch the military jets come in to land over the Alde to realise that some of the changes have little in common with the intrinsic character of the area. As we approach the end of the 20th century, the pace of change seems to quicken and the threats to the special qualities of the Suffolk Coast and Heaths landscape appear more real than ever. Unless these pressures are recognised and positively controlled and managed, it is possible that they could have significant and long lasting effects. The main prospects for change seem likely to arise from:

- improvements to the A12 that may improve accessibility to the area and possibly increasing pressure from visitors and for further housing development;
- development pressure, including the demand for new or extended homes that may be out of character with the landscape;
- changes from agricultural to recreational use by, for example the development of golf courses and the increased use of land for keeping horses;

- growing pressure for water-related recreation, including demands for additional marinas and yacht moorings, the increasing popularity of noisy water sports such as water-skiing and jet-skiing;
- uncertainties regarding the future of Woodbridge and Bentwaters airfields, and the potential impact of further development to make use of redundant infrastructure;
- the development of a third reactor at Sizewell nuclear power station;
- the possible effects of sea-level rise, including the need to improve flood defences and the consequent pressures on saltings and mudflats;
- the continued loss of traditional landscape elements including hedgerows, lines of trees marking changes in slope and individual trees;
- further changes in agricultural practices including the introduction of new crops, the increase in open-air pig farming, the wider use of plastic sheeting to aid early crop growth, the use of intensive irrigation techniques and the design and location of agricultural buildings;
- management of the landscape to re-create heathland and marsh where in the past they have been reclaimed for agriculture.

Conclusions

This chapter has demonstrated that the landscape of the Suffolk Coast and Heaths is of a quality that warrants its designation as an AONB. In essence, it is a landscape of variety and contrast, the coast and estuaries framing a mosaic of marshes, meres, heathland, woods and forests and farmland. Much of the area's special quality can be attributed to the special character of individual landscape types, but equally important are the contrasts and transitions that occur between them. Although views along the coast and estuaries are often long, the gentle, rolling landform means that views inland are often contained, and the scene constantly changes as one moves through the countryside. The wild and remote coast contrasts with the peace and tranquillity of the sheltered estuaries. The historic towns and villages, the isolated churches and the scatter of farms each reflecting the local vernacular, are an integral part of this landscape and make an essential contribution to its character.

Management of the AONB must reflect the essential character of the Suffolk Coast and Heaths, aiming to promote policies that reinforce this

High tide forms a tranquil lake at Blythburgh.

character, and resisting changes that threaten to undermine it. The emphasis, therefore, should be on conserving, rather than preserving the landscape, maximising the opportunities for enhancement. Already we see policies designed to reverse the more severe effects of past agricultural improvements, for instance re-creating heathland in the sandlings and re-establishing marshes where they were previously drained. The range of local authorities and other agencies that are active in the area clearly have an important role to play in conserving and enhancing the landscape, applying strong policies to restrict

unsuitable development. The AONB management plan, which is being prepared for the area, will be critical in establishing policies, and coordinating and directing actions. Only through such concerted effort will the essential qualities of this nationally important landscape be conserved and enhanced for future generations to enjoy.

"Long have I loved thee Mother Suffolk, dear,
More than the heart can know or tongue can tell,
In rivers winding slow, in reedy mere,
In sandy heathlands and deepwooded dell."

Alistair Davis [27].

REFERENCES

1. Countryside Commission (1987), *Landscape assessment: A Countryside Commission approach*, CCD 18, Countryside Commission, Cheltenham.

2. Beardall, C H et al (1991), *The Suffolk estuaries: A report by the Suffolk Wildlife Trust on the wildlife and conservation of the Suffolk estuaries*, Segment Publications, Colchester.

3. Ryece, R (1618), *The breviary of Suffolk*, Ed. Hervey Lord F (1903).

4. Chadwick, L (1982), *In search of heathland*, Dennis Dobson, London and Durham.

5. Arnott, W G (1952), *Alde estuary: The story of a Suffolk river*, Norman Adlard and Co, Ipswich.

6. Young, A (1794), *General view of the agriculture of the county of Suffolk*, David and Charles, Newton Abbott, Devon (1969).

7. Holst, I (1966), *Britten*, London.

8. Innes, H (1986), *East Anglia*, Hodder and Stoughton, London.

9. Arnott, W G (1954), *Orwell estuary: The story of Ipswich river*, Boydwell Press, Ipswich.

10. Arnott, W G (1950), *Suffolk estuary: The story of the River Deben*, Norman Adlard and Co, Ipswich.

11. Gissing, G (1903), 'The private papers of Henry Ryecroft' cited by Jebb, M (1990), *East Anglia: an anthology*, The National Trust, London.

12. Scarfe, N (1976), *Suffolk, A Shell Guide*, Faber and Faber, London.

13. Tennyson, J (1939), *Suffolk scene: A book of description and adventure*, Blackie and Son Ltd, London and Glasgow.

14. Pennington, J (1950), 'East Anglia' in *The British countryside in colour*, Odhams, London.

15. Turner, J (1977), *The countryside of Britain*, Ward Lock, London.

16. Kirby, J (1735), *The Suffolk Traveller*.

17. Dymond, D (1989), 'The landscape' in Jennings, C (1989), *Suffolk for ever*, Alastair Press, Suffolk.

18. Young, A (1771), *The Farmer's tour through the east of England*, London.

19. Blyth, R (1989), 'Our villages' in Jennings *op cit*.

20. Fitch, J (1989), 'The churches – and their future' in Jennings *op cit*.

21. Crabbe, G (1967), 'The village' and 'The borough' in *Tales, 1812 and other poems*, Cambridge.

22. Drayton, M (1622), 'Poly-Olbion' in *The works of Michael Drayton*, London (1876).

23. Engleheart, F (1965), 'Pin Mill' in *A selection of poetry*, Norman Adlard and Co, Ipswich.

24. Seago, E (1947), *A canvas to cover*, London.

25. Dutt, W (1923), *A guide to the Norfolk Broads*, London (cited by Jebb, M (1990)).

26. Terhune, A M (1980), *The letters of Edward Fitzgerald*, Princeton, Guildford.

27. Davis, A (nd), quoted in Arnott (1952) *op cit*.

ACKNOWLEDGEMENTS

We should like to acknowledge the many organisations and individuals who helped us in the preparation of this report. In particular we should like to thank the staff of Suffolk and Essex County Councils, and Suffolk Coastal, Babergh, Waveney and Tendring District Councils. Thanks are due to Dr Peter Howard of the University of Plymouth for assistance with research concerning art. We also appreciated the support of Tim De-Keyzer of the Countryside Commission's Eastern Regional Office.

The Land Use Consultants project team was Carys Swanwick, Nick James and Jane Fowles. The watercolour and pencil illustrations are by Jane Fowles.

All photographs are by David Burton Associates, except those on pages 11, 16, 17, 21, 24, 27, 28, 31, 33, which are by Land Use Consultants.

THE LINCOLNSHIRE WOLDS LANDSCAPE

A landscape assessment prepared by
Cobham Resource Consultants
for the Countryside Commission.

Distributed by:
Countryside Commission Postal Sales
PO Box 124
Walgrave
Northampton NN6 9TL
Telephone: 0604 781848

© Countryside Commission 1993
CCP 414
ISBN 0 86170 378 2
Price £7.00

CONTENTS

FIGURES

British Library Cataloguing-in-Publication data.
A catalogue record for this book is available from the British Library.

Cover: *The Lincolnshire Wolds near Belchford* (Lincolnshire County Council)

Designed and printed by H.E. Boddy & Co. Ltd., Banbury.
Maps produced by The Edge, Cheltenham.

The Lincolnshire Wolds rise up from the surrounding fens, coastal marshland and the Vale of Lincoln. It is a quiet, sparsely settled area with wide views over rolling hills and intimate valleys. It is the special nature of this chalk upland, so much shaped by the hand of man that led to its designation in 1973 as an Area of Outstanding Natural Beauty.

The Countryside Commission wants to increase understanding and to raise awareness of the area's importance locally and nationally. It therefore asked Cobham Resource Consultants to prepare this assessment of the landscape character and quality of the Lincolnshire Wolds.

This report will help to promote further debate and action to conserve the Lincolnshire Wolds. The Commission looks forward to continuing to develop this work in partnership with the local authorities and others who have a role to play in the management of the area.

Sir John Johnson
Chairman
Countryside Commission

The Lincolnshire Wolds Area of Outstanding Natural Beauty (AONB) extends from near Grimsby in the north to Horncastle in the south, and represents the highest ground for many miles around in this remote, rather isolated corner of England. Over the 20 years of designation there have been significant landscape changes. In recent years there has also been considerable action by the local authorities, landowners and others to direct and manage landscape change in a positive way.

The primary purpose of this landscape assessment is to identify and describe the basis for designation, that is the special character and national importance of the Lincolnshire Wolds landscape. A whole range of factors contributes to the area's outstanding natural beauty, including scenic quality, geology, topography, flora, fauna, historical and cultural factors.

The assessment also aims to raise awareness of the AONB, and to guide and influence those responsible for its policies and management. It is intended to be a key reference source for the Lincolnshire Wolds AONB Forum. This group includes representatives of the local authorities; farming, forestry and rural development interests; and wildlife and amenity bodies. It has a central role in the conservation and enhancement of the Wolds landscape and in future will be responsible for the preparation and implementation of a detailed AONB management plan.

The method of landscape assessment has been based on Countryside Commission guidelines and has included research and desk study of background material, analysis of map data, and field survey work. In addition, meetings have been held with acknowledged local experts and members of the Lincolnshire Wolds AONB Forum to review pressures on the landscape and to assess future change.

The report includes:
- an introduction to the physical and human influences that have shaped the Lincolnshire Wolds landscape;
- a description of the landscape character of the Wolds, and how that character varies across the AONB;
- details of how the landscape has been perceived and appreciated over the centuries;
- a review of landscape change, and how it may affect the area's scenic quality in future, together with suggestions for the management of different landscape types and features;
- a statement about the special qualities of the area, including a summary of the reasons why it is of national importance.

Cobham Resource Consultants
June 1993

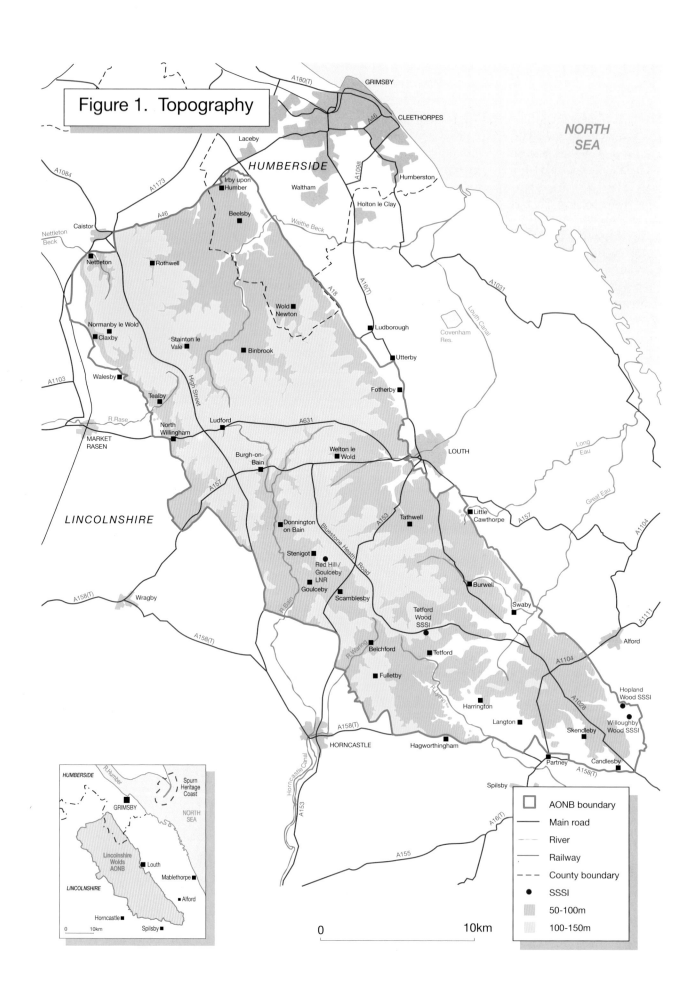

Figure 1. Topography

NORTH SEA

HUMBERSIDE

LINCOLNSHIRE

GRIMSBY
CLEETHORPES
Laceby
Irby upon Humber
Waltham
Humberston
Holton le Clay
Beelsby
Waithe Beck
A1084
A1173
A46
Caistor
Nettleton Beck
Nettleton
Rothwell
Wold Newton
Ludborough
Louth Canal
Covenham Res.
A18
A16(T)
A1031
Normanby le Wold
Claxby
Stainton le Vale
Binbrook
Utterby
High Street
A1103
Walesby
Tealby
Fotherby
R.Rase
North Willingham
Ludford
A631
MARKET RASEN
Burgh-on-Bain
Welton le Wold
LOUTH
Long Eau
A157
Little Cawthorpe
A157
A1104
Donnington on Bain
Tathwell
A153
Stenigot
Bluestone Heath Road
Red Hill / Goulceby LNR
Goulceby
Scamblesby
Burwell
Swaby
R.Bain
Wragby
A158(T)
Tetford Wood SSSI
Alford
A1104
A1111
R.Waring
Belchford
Tetford
A158(T)
Hopland Wood SSSI
Fulletby
R.Lymn
Harrington
A1028
Langton
Willoughby Wood SSSI
Skendleby
HORNCASTLE
Hagworthingham
Candlesby
Partney
A158(T)
Horncastle Canal
Spilsby
A153
A16(T)
A155

Inset map:
HUMBERSIDE
R.Humber
Spurn Heritage Coast
GRIMSBY
NORTH SEA
Lincolnshire Wolds AONB
Louth
LINCOLNSHIRE
Mablethorpe
Alford
Horncastle
Spilsby
0   10km

Legend:
☐ AONB boundary
— Main road
— River
— Railway
--- County boundary
● SSSI
▨ 50-100m
▨ 100-150m

0   10km

4

The Lincolnshire Wolds lie in the north-eastern quarter of the county of Lincolnshire, mid-way between Lincoln and the coast (Figure 1). Rising to over 150 m along their western edge, the Wolds form the highest ground in eastern England between Yorkshire and Kent. To the west, they overlook the Vale of Lincoln, with distant views of Lincoln Cathedral; while to the east, they are separated from the North Sea by a wide band of low-lying coastal marshland. To the north lies the River Humber, and to the south, the Lincolnshire Fens and the Wash. Closely settled and farmed for hundreds of years, these swelling uplands possess a gentle charm. Their scenery is characterised by open hill tops, sweeping views, wide grass verges, wooded slopes and valleys, and ancient half-hidden villages.

The impetus for designation as an AONB came originally from the Council for the Protection of Rural England and from Lindsey County Council — the planning authority responsible for the area prior to local government reorganisation in 1974. In an AONB Statement of Intent published in 1971 [1], the County Council requested that the Countryside Commission designate the Lincolnshire Wolds as an AONB under Section 87 of the National Parks and Access to the Countryside Act. The designation was confirmed in 1973, and covers an area of 558 sq km, mainly within the present-day county of Lincolnshire. However, a small proportion of the AONB, in the north-east corner, falls within Humberside. The designated area is approximately 45 km long by 15 km wide, and is bounded by the towns of Market Rasen to the west, Louth to the east, Caistor to the north, and Horncastle and Spilsby to the south.

Among the forces that have shaped the Lincolnshire Wolds landscape, there are two particularly strong influences. The first is the very varied underlying geology, which in turn has been subject to complex glacial processes. Without a basic understanding of these physical factors, it is difficult to make sense of the area's present-day landform and drainage, which are strikingly different from those of other wolds landscapes elsewhere in England. The second influence is the long continuity of farming and settlement. Unlike certain other AONBs, which contain large areas of wild land, much of the Wolds is in intensive agricultural use, and has been for centuries. Far from detracting from the area's scenic interest, its history as a 'working landscape' has led to the creation of many fine and distinctive landscape patterns and features.

Physical influences

Physical features and geology

The physical features of the Lincolnshire Wolds, as shown in Figure 2, is dominated by a west-facing chalk escarpment. Geologically, this escarpment is an outcrop of the same strata that form the Yorkshire Wolds to the north, and the Chilterns and Berkshire Downs to the south. However, in Lincolnshire its form is much more complex. The Chalk here is only about 50 m thick, so that although Chalk caps the hills, the underlying Lower Cretaceous strata are revealed on much of the scarp face and in the bottoms of the deeper valleys. In the southern third of the AONB, the Chalk has largely been removed, and the Lower Cretaceous sands, clays and ironstones form a secondary series of ridges to the west and south of the Chalk. Both the Chalk and the Lower Cretaceous rocks have been extensively moulded by glacial and periglacial action that has significantly altered the drainage pattern and left widespread, superficial deposits of Boulder Clay, especially in the south. On the eastern edge of the Wolds there is no simple dip slope, but a clear sharp edge that represents former sea cliffs, now masked by glacial till.

The west-facing chalk escarpment, from which there are extensive views over the Vale of Lincoln.

Figure 3 presents, in simplified form, the solid and drift geology of the Wolds [2, 3]. In general terms, the northern part of the area is a smooth, rolling chalk plateau, with thin soils. Between Caistor and Market Rasen there is a steep, prominent, west-facing escarpment that at its highest point around Normanby le Wold, reaches 168 m above sea-level. The bulk of the scarp face comprises Lower Cretaceous rocks, with successive exposure of thin beds of Red Chalk, Carstone, Roach, Tealby Clay and Limestone, Claxby Ironstone and Spilsby Sandstone. As a result, the

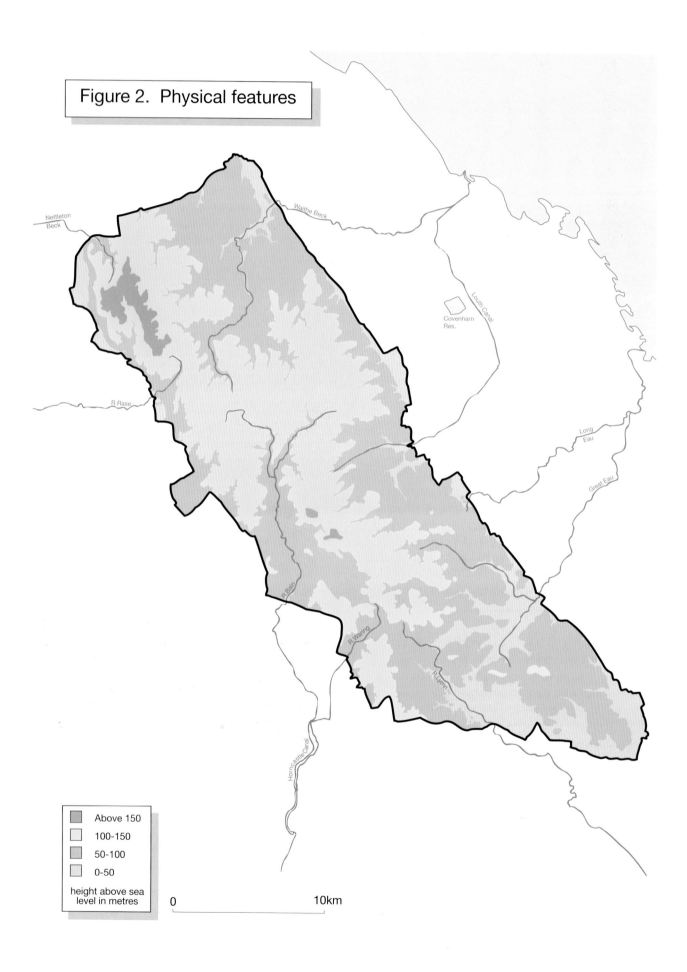

Figure 2. Physical features

Nettleton Beck

Waithe Beck

Louth Canal

Covenham Res.

R.Rase

Long Eau

Great Eau

R.Bain

R.Waring

R.Lymn

Horncastle Canal

	Above 150
	100-150
	50-100
	0-50

height above sea
level in metres

0   10km

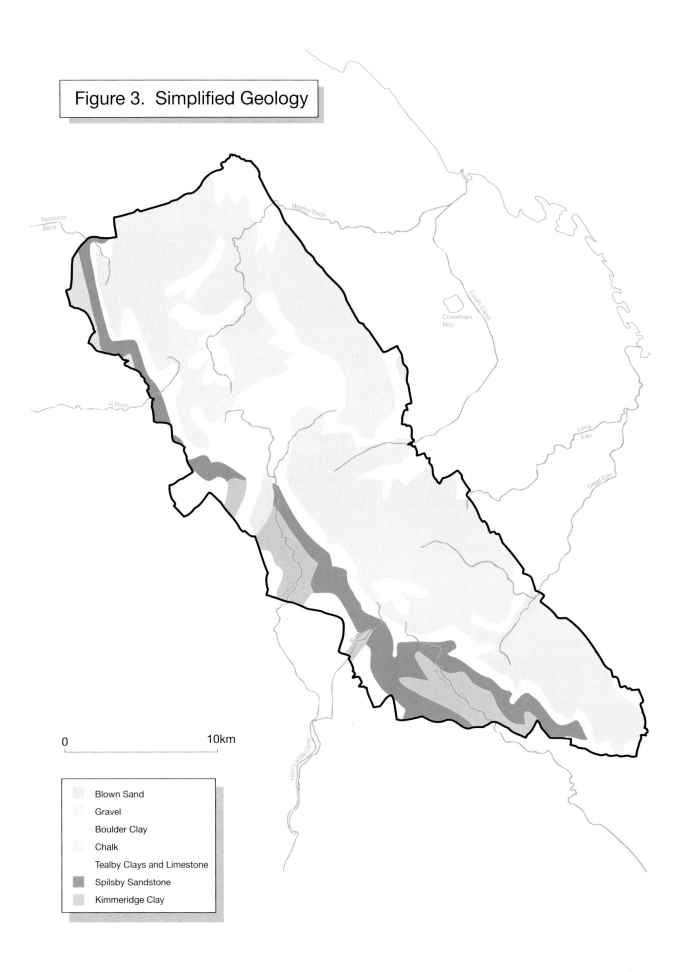

Figure 3. Simplified Geology

Nettleton Beck

Waithe Beck

Louth Canal

Covenham Res.

R.Rase

Long Eau

Great Eau

R.Bain

R.Waring

R.Lymn

Horncastle Canal

0   10km

Blown Sand
Gravel
Boulder Clay
Chalk
Tealby Clays and Limestone
Spilsby Sandstone
Kimmeridge Clay

Figure 4. Extract from sheet 103 geology map

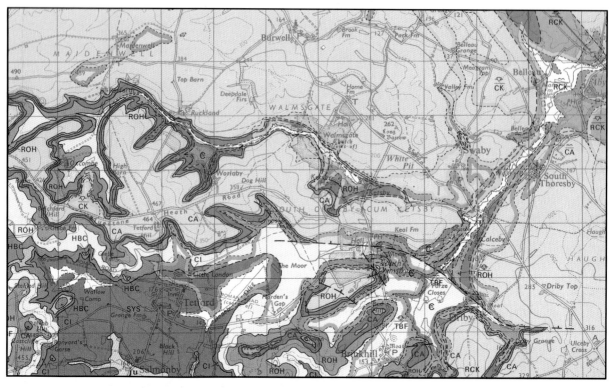

Scale   1:50000

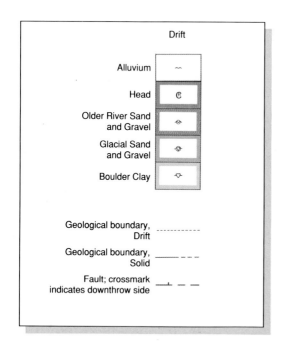

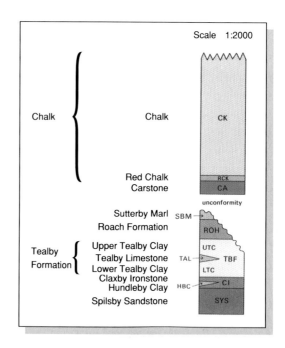

Chalk caps the tops of the Wolds, but deposits are thin, and the underlying strata are often exposed on the scarp face and in the deeper valleys.

Glaciation

Glaciation of the Lincolnshire Wolds has given rise to some of the area's most striking landscape features. The history of glaciation is immensely complicated [4, 5], but the basic story is clear. The last main (penultimate) glaciation of the British Isles took place around 200,000–150,000 years ago. Ice moved south and covered most of the Lincolnshire Wolds, smoothing and moulding the northern part of the escarpment, as well as leaving large deposits of chalky till. The last interglacial period that followed, saw a massive rise in sea-level. This truncated the dip slope of the Wolds and produced what must have been an impressive line of chalk cliffs, along the eastern edge of the area. The main incision of the Wolds river valleys also took place at this time. For instance, the headwaters of Nettleton Beck and the River Bain [6] cut into the chalk escarpment, and their valleys were probably also deepened by glacial melt-waters. To the east and south, Waithe Beck, the Lud system, the Great Eau and the Lymn established courses similar to those of the present day.

The most influential period for the Lincolnshire Wolds landscape was the final glaciation, which reached its peak around 70,000 years ago. At that time, the Wolds formed a tundra island surrounded by ice to the east and water to the west and south. As the ice began to melt, lakes and spillways formed along the eastern side of the Wolds. The main drainage was to the south, where vast deltas of outwash sands and gravels were created within the valleys of the Bain and the Lymn. To the east, the exit of water was often blocked by ice, forcing the melt-waters to escape across valley divides into other catchments.

These forces led to the creation of at least 70 or 80 glacial melt-water channels, mainly in the southern and eastern wolds. Some form almost gorge-like features that still carry rivers; others are now deep, rounded dry valleys. Permanent diversion of streams often occurred, for example at Hubbard's Hills, south-west of Louth, where the original valley was blocked by glacial till, and the river cut a gorge northwards to join another valley. Where major rivers were blocked, large ponded-lake systems developed. The most extensive systems were along Waithe Beck in the north, within the valleys of the Lud and its tributaries near Louth, and at Calceby in the south. Here the headwaters of the Great Eau (Calceby Beck) backed up and eventually overflowed southwards into the Lymn catchment through the spectacular New England gorge. Such lake and spillway features are very prominent within the landscape. Typically the headwaters cut down into the Lower Cretaceous series to form deep, dramatic valleys within the Wolds plateau, surrounded by huge, rolling chalk hillsides, often floored with heavier soils. These systems can be seen very clearly at 1:50,000 scale on solid and drift geology maps. Figure 4 shows an example.

face is characterised by land slips and slumping, has a hummocky appearance, and is largely uncultivated. It is dissected by several streams (for instance Nettleton Beck) that cut back into the scarp and form deep valleys behind, and parallel to, the main escarpment. Hence there is effectively a double escarpment, with the first continuous ridge lying some two to three kilometres east of the main scarp face. The main tops of the Wolds, in this northern half, are drained in an easterly direction by Waithe Beck, the headwaters of which have cut down to the Lower Cretaceous rocks. On the eastern margin of the area, between Laceby and Louth, rounded chalk hills, broken by short, steep-sided valleys, descend sharply to the coastal claylands below.

In the southern Wolds, the chalk escarpment is much less prominent. It becomes an internal feature, extending south-eastward from Donington through Red Hill and Tetford to Langton. It overlooks to the south a ridge of Lower Cretaceous rocks capped by Boulder Clay. The dominant rock here is the Spilsby Sandstone occurring at the surface over wide areas, particularly around the Lymn Valley where it gives rise to acid soils. In the south-west there are outliers of Chalk and Roach, forming low hills and knolls above the surrounding countryside. This whole southern section of the Wolds is dominated by two main north–south river systems, the Bain and the Lymn. Their broad valleys are floored by Kimmeridge Clay, part of the Upper Jurassic series, which lies beneath the Spilsby Sandstone. The south-eastern edge of the area, from Louth to Candlesby, is blanketed by Boulder Clay, giving a very gentle, rounded landform, broken only by the deep valleys of the Lud above Louth, and the Great Eau at Calceby.

This valley, near Thoresway in the northern Wolds, is part of the Waithe Beck system and is an example of the deep, rolling valleys formed by glacial melt-waters.

As in earlier periods, the last glaciation resulted in massive deposition of glacial sands, gravels and boulder clays. Along the ice margin to the east of the Wolds, low hummocky moraines and outwash gravels were laid down. The former cliff line was obscured by till, and boulder clays were also deposited over wide areas – particularly in the south-east.

Soils and land use

The soils and land use patterns of the Lincolnshire Wolds are a close reflection of the area's complex solid and drift geology [7]. In the northern Wolds, the plateau tops are dominated by light, chalky soils. On the valley sides, where the rivers have cut through to the underlying Red Chalk and Lower Cretaceous series, the soils may show striking variations in colour and texture. In the south-east, the chalky boulder clays give rise to heavy, seasonally waterlogged soils; while around the Lymn Valley, where the drift deposits have been removed by subsequent fluvial action, the Spilsby Sandstone provides the parent material for well-drained, sandy loams. On the floor of the Bain Valley, glacial sands and gravels produce deep, coarse, generally permeable loams. However, the impermeable Kimmeridge Clays, which lie below, give rise locally to areas of high water table.

The vast majority of the Lincolnshire Wolds AONB is Grade 2 agricultural land. This is concentrated, particularly, on the plateau tops where productivity is good but constrained by the thin, droughty nature of the chalk soils. Most of these areas are in permanent arable use. The valley floors, with their heavy and sometimes waterlogged soils, are generally Grade 3 land, and are often under woodland or pasture. There are small areas of Grade 4, mainly along the northern scarp face, where the land is in rough pasture or scrub. Overall, more than 80 per cent of the AONB is in arable use, the main crops being winter wheat, winter barley, oil seed rape, winter beans, and linseed. Between 10 and 15 per cent of land (essentially the steeper slopes and heavier soils) is used as permanent pasture for sheep or cattle. Only two to three per cent of land cover is woodland: a very low figure by national standards.

Human influences

Prehistoric and Roman times

The Lincolnshire Wolds are known to have been inhabited from the post-glacial, Palaeolithic period onwards and indeed the oldest human remains in Britain were discovered within the Wolds. However, it is unlikely that there was significant human settlement until the Mesolithic period, which lasted from approximately 10,000 to 4,500 BC. At this time the heavy claylands of the Wolds would have been covered with dense forest of oak, alder and lime, with open woodland and heathland on the chalk tops above. Mesolithic activity was almost certainly concentrated on the higher, drier ground, and a concentration of sites occurs on the Spilsby Sandstone at the southern end of the Wolds.

Later, in the Neolithic, Bronze and Iron Ages, settlement extended onto the chalk, at least in the southern Wolds [8]. The northern Wolds appear to have been less populated, perhaps because there are fewer surface streams. The remains of prehistoric settlement are quite visible in some parts of the Wolds, for instance at Skendleby, where there is a prominent group of Neolithic long barrows; and near Burgh on Bain and elsewhere where Bronze Age round barrows cap the hill tops. Prehistoric settlement was initially related to hunting and gathering, followed by a mix of pastoral use and shifting cultivation, and more permanent settlement and woodland clearance from the Iron Age onwards. By the time of the Roman invasion it is likely that the chalk uplands were reasonably open country, with well-established ancient trackways along the ridge and a network of local routeways (that today form green lanes) in the south [9]. The main trackways were High Street, which runs north–south along the chalk escarpment from Caistor; the Bluestone Heath Road, which follows the chalk ridge south-eastward from the central Wolds to Calceby; and Barton Street, which follows the old cliff line along the eastern edge of the Wolds. Today, Barton Street acts as the boundary of the AONB along much of its eastern edge.

The Romans were active in the Wolds, although relatively few signs of Roman habitation survive. In the southern part of the AONB, the line of a Roman road that joined Lincoln to the coast can still be traced through Tetford and north of Skendleby. East–west roads were also built to serve the coastal salt industry — the road that crosses the Wolds through Tathwell, south of Louth, is a good example of such a salters' road. A walled town was established at Caistor; and a fort at Horncastle. During Roman times the northern and central Wolds appear to have become important farming areas with several large villas, such as that at Ludford.

Saxon and medieval settlement

The major, permanent settlement of the Wolds took place from Saxon times onwards. Many of the area's villages have Saxon origins, and the Saxon and later Danish settlements and farming practices created many of the parish boundaries that survive to this day. Place names provide a clue to the distribution of settlement. Villages including 'ham' and 'ton' probably have Saxon origins; while names ending in 'by' or 'thorpe' suggest Danish settlement. Different farming systems were favoured by the two peoples. In general, the Saxons were cultivators and settled mainly in the north and centre, where there is a pattern of large parishes. In the south, there was a concentration of Danish settlement, with smaller parishes and pastoral land use on the poorer clay and sandstone soils [10].

By *Domesday*, it seems that almost all of the Wolds was in agricultural use, under the open field system, although substantial areas of woodland survived in the Bain Valley and along the eastern edge of the Wolds south of Louth [11]. On the high tops there are believed to have been monastic grange farms belonging to the Cistercian abbey at Louth Park. Here sheep would have been bred, and then moved down to the coastal marsh for fattening. The Wolds as a whole supported a dense population, and there was an extensive network of nucleated villages.

However, from the 12th century onwards, widespread depopulation and village desertion took place [12]. The legacy of this period can still be seen in the huge number of deserted medieval villages within the Wolds, for instance at Calcethorpe and Fordington. There seem to have been many reasons for village abandonment. During the 12th century, civil war and the expansion of the monastic granges probably had an influence. In the late 14th century, the population was badly hit by the Black Death. After around 1450, when the most widespread depopulation occurred, the main factor was the demand for wool by the expanding English cloth industry, at a time when the post-plague population had not recovered sufficiently to increase the demand for corn. This led to some deliberate village clearances to permit enclosure to sheep walk. From around 1520, as the population again expanded, enclosure was undertaken to permit improved arable farming. A much more open and sparsely populated landscape was created, with large fields and wide expanses of downland grazed by sheep. As in the Cotswolds, much of the medieval wool wealth went towards building churches and dwellings for prosperous yeomen.

Parliamentary enclosures

Between the 16th and 18th centuries, agriculture in the Lincolnshire Wolds again suffered decline. During this period, it seems that parts of the area reverted to heath and wasteland. Unusually, large areas were given over to rabbit warrens, with commercial rearing and trapping for fur. Although warrens were found throughout Lincolnshire, there was a particular concentration on the light chalk soils of the Wolds escarpment [13].

By the latter part of the 18th century several factors combined to encourage agricultural intensification. New agricultural techniques were available. Rapid population growth, industrialisation and urbanisation were taking place. With the outbreak of the Napoleonic Wars, there was a need for self-sufficiency in food production.

At this time, much of the Lincolnshire Wolds area was still farmed under the old open field system. There were relatively few large estates as a strong tradition of free peasantry prevailed. Although many parishes contained medieval enclosures, especially close to the villages, wide areas were either common pasture or huge open fields.

In the 70 years from 1760 to 1830, this landscape was utterly transformed by the parliamentary enclosures. Some fascinating examples of the changes that occurred are presented in a book entitled *Old and new landscapes in the Horncastle area* [14]. The authors highlight the contrast between pre- and post-enclosure field patterns and landscape features. Open unhedged fields and commons were planted with literally hundreds of kilometres of hawthorn hedges. New Georgian manors, parks and farmsteads were established, often away from the villages. Small game coverts, parkland, tree belts and avenues were planted within the previously open landscape, and on some estates hunting and shooting became popular pastimes. Straight drove roads up to 20 m in width were built, between newly planted hedges. The verges provided grazing for the flocks of sheep that were driven across the Wolds to the coastal grazing marshes. An intensive cropping system was established, with a four-course rotation made possible by applications of manure, bone meal and chalk or lime extracted locally from small chalk pits [15].

Later in the 19th century, increasing agricultural prosperity, the introduction of steam power to the farm, and large-scale food production and storage, led to the construction of extensive, planned farmsteads. These Victorian farm complexes were built both in the villages and in the open countryside, for example at Rothwell, Binbrook, Stainton le Vale and Stenigot. Often there was associated estate housing for tenants and farm workers, for example at Wold Newton.

The landscape that we see today is largely a product of the parliamentary enclosures, although subsequent 20th century influences have included wartime airfields, continuing arable intensification, mineral extraction, new roads and housing. This present-day landscape is described in the next chapter.

Wide roadside verges of the drove roads were established during the parliamentary enclosures, and today form an important remnant of undisturbed, herb-rich ancient grassland.

2. THE CHARACTER OF THE LANDSCAPE TODAY

In assessing the character of the Lincolnshire Wolds today, we have found it helpful to consider the landscape from several different perspectives. Primarily we have looked upon it as a scenic resource, and hence its visual character is described in some detail. However, we recognise that it also presents many distinctive features of conservation interest, including sites and habitats of nature conservation value, archaeological and historic landscape features, and buildings and settlements. Hence these aspects of landscape character are also described. Together all these strands contribute to the unique 'sense of place' that is the Wolds.

The Lincolnshire Wolds have a strong unity of visual character, resulting from the physical and human influences described earlier. Common qualities across the area are the enormous views; the open sweeping landform and ridge-top routeways; the seasonally changing colours and textures of the fields; and the deep, dramatic wooded valleys. However, there are also considerable variations in

scenic character across the Wolds, and an understanding of these variations is essential as a basis for future landscape conservation and enhancement.

Differences in landscape character reflect many factors, but in the Lincolnshire Wolds it is the topography and geology that appear to be the dominant factors. In simple terms, there are four landscape character areas within the Wolds (Figure 5). In the northern half of the AONB, the escarpment landscapes of the north western edge may be distinguished from the chalk wolds landscapes that lie to the east and extend southwards through the centre of the AONB. Locally, these wolds landscapes have been much modified by glaciation and contain intimate valley features contrasting strongly with the open tops. In the south-west, the influence of the Lower Cretaceous rocks creates an unusual ridge and valley landscape, which is clearly separated from the eastward facing, wooded claylands south of Louth. These four areas are described below.

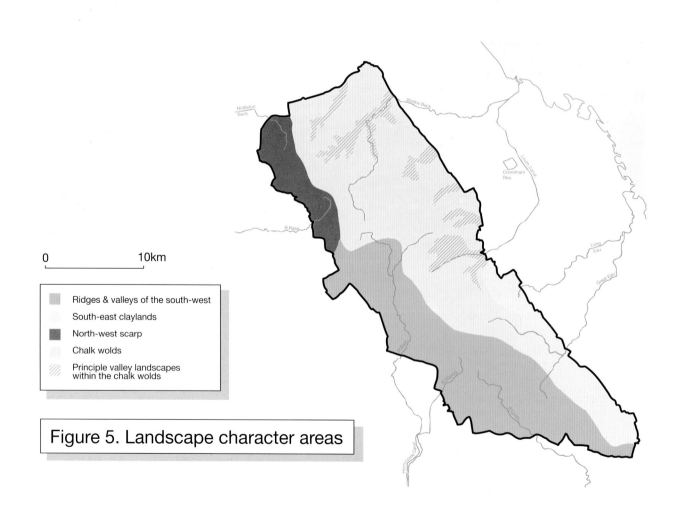

0   10km

Ridges & valleys of the south-west
South-east claylands
North-west scarp
Chalk wolds
Principle valley landscapes within the chalk wolds

Figure 5. Landscape character areas

The north-west scarp

The north-west scarp.

In the north, the western edge of the Lincolnshire Wolds is marked by a clear chalk scarp, visible for some distance as a vertical feature in an otherwise flat landscape. This pronounced escarpment, with exposed scars of white and red chalk and outcrops of ironstone, extends from Caistor south to North Willingham. The rounded hills of the main scarp face are largely in rough pasture, although there are also wedges of woodland, areas of scrub and remains of ironstone workings. The slopes present a steep and hummocky appearance, indented by spring lines. At the foot of the scarp are a number of attractive small villages, including Nettleton, Walesby, and Tealby.

Buildings in ironstone and Tealby Limestone, such as the fine hill top medieval church at Walesby, are distinctive of this area, whereas brick is more typical elsewhere. At the top of the scarp there are commanding views to the north and west. These are particularly dramatic between Normanby le Wold and Nettleton, where there is a real sense of being on top of the world.

To the east of the main scarp face are the parallel valleys of Nettleton Beck, Usselby Beck and the River Rase, which in turn are backed by a second, somewhat higher ridge along the line of High Street. The valley at

Much of the north-west scarp is in rough pasture and scrub. Its slopes are indented by spring lines, as seen here near Normanby le Wold.

The old church at Walesby is built in Tealby Limestone and forms a well-known landmark on the hill top above the village.

Nettleton Beck is an open landscape, with scrubby grassland, a number of quarries and a landfill that detract from the landscape locally. Within the valleys, small deciduous woodlands typically cap the steepest slopes and run along the valley bottoms where they cut through the chalk.

Ancient trackways follow many Lincolnshire Wold ridges, the tops of which are marked by prehistoric tumuli, and by attractive clumps of beech trees, often dating from the time of the parliamentary enclosures.

High Street forms the eastern edge of the character area. This gently winding ancient trackway is now a quiet, minor road, with open, westward views along most of its length. There is little settlement along the road, bar a few scattered farmsteads. Hill crests along the road are frequently marked by tumuli and attractive clumps of beech. However, large, modern farm buildings and radio masts detract from the landscape in some areas.

The chalk wolds

The chalk wolds – the tops.

This landscape character area extends over a large portion of the northern and central Wolds. It is mainly an open, arable plain. Within the plain, though, there are dramatic, rolling, inward-facing valley and dry valley features, representing the glacial lakes and spillways that covered wide areas of the Lincolnshire Wolds at the end of the last glaciation. These two types of landscape are intimately linked and indeed the contrast between the arable tops and the lush, wooded valleys is one of the special qualities of the chalk wolds landscape.

Entering the area from High Street to the west, one is conscious that the land dips gently eastward. Most of the roads also run eastward along low ridgelines. Many of these are wide, droving roads that date from the time of the parliamentary enclosures and are lined with fine hedgerow plantings of ash and beech. Although most of the land is in intensive arable use, shallow valleys lie below marked by valley woodlands, sited on heavier soils, for example near Stainton le Vale.

In the northern part of the area there are two very strong valley landscapes, around Rothwell and Cuxwold on Laceby Beck, and around Thoresway, Thorganby and Hatcliffe on Waithe Beck and its tributaries. At Rothwell, the estate owners have clearly stamped their mark upon the surrounding countryside, through unusual, tall, A-shaped hedges, widespread planting of hedgerow trees, and banks of daffodils along the road verges. At Thoresway and elsewhere within the intimate valleys there is a sense of a much older landscape than on the tops. This perception is based on fact, for the valleys do indeed contain villages of Saxon and medieval origin, ancient winding lanes and trackways, lush mixed hedgerows, and many other pre-enclosure landscape features.

South of Binbrook, the same rolling landform occurs, but here it is not marked by woodland to the same degree, and hence the valleys are much less prominent visually. In addition, the former RAF Binbrook airfield and associated housing spread their influence over a wide area. This very

The chalk wolds are distinguished by the strong sense of contrast between their lush valley landscapes and the open tops above. This view towards the village for Stainton le Vale also shows Binbrook airfield on the high ground.

open, exposed, intensively arable character extends eastward to North Elkington and south to Burwell, where the whole central spine of the Wolds is flat or gently undulating, with enormous fields, few woods or tall hedgerows, and very sparse settlement. In parts it is adversely affected by disused wartime airfields, transmission lines, radio masts, and huge straw stacks that in places dominate the skyline on the scale of factory buildings. However, it is also a simple, boldly patterned landscape, punctuated by isolated farmsteads and small plantations. There are huge expanses of field and sky, and fine outward views, for example westwards from High Street near Ludford Magna, and eastward from the Bluestone Heath Road above Louth. Within this area also there are many signs of early habitation, including long barrows, tumuli, deserted medieval villages and small chalk pits from which lime was extracted for agricultural purposes.

Along the whole eastern edge of the chalk wolds, the open chalkland and the valley landscapes are closely juxtaposed, as a series of short, steep valleys cut through the former cliff line, which is clearly marked and offers long views over the marshes below. Lush valley landscapes can be found around Hatcliffe, Beesby, North Ormsby, and in particular to the west of Louth. Again, the valleys contain ancient villages, hedgerows, woodland, pasture and many pre-enclosure landscape features. Most villages include a hall or manor, often surrounded by parkland. Above the villages, the spurs of chalkland that overlook the marsh are often crowned by prehistoric earthworks and clumps of beech.

The rolling nature of the landform, created by the glacial melt-waters having deepened valleys, creates a 'roller coaster' effect.

The ridges and valleys of the south-west

The ridges and valleys of the south-west scarp.

The Bluestone Heath Road, which runs south-eastward across the Wolds, marks a clear change in landscape character. The road follows the edge of the chalk outcrop. To the south and west the topography and geology — and hence the landscape — are much more complex. In general, the landform is fragmented and angular, with sharp ridges and outliers of the more resistant Lower Cretaceous rocks, capped by Boulder Clay, running north-west to south-east above the valleys of the Rivers Bain and Lymn. The chalk ridge is marked by deep combes, for example at Oxcombe, and by many spillway features, notably where the Great Eau and Calceby Beck have breached the chalk ridge. South of Tetford the New England valley cuts deeply through the Spilsby Sandstone.

Oxcombe is one of a series of deep valleys and combes viewed from the chalk ridge.

In general, this is a more wooded, enclosed, pastoral and settled landscape than the landscapes further north — reflecting, perhaps, its links with the Danish people. The influence of the parliamentary enclosures is less obvious, with generally smaller fields and a more complicated, narrow, winding road network. There is a mix of arable farming, and cattle and sheep rearing.

In some areas such as at Stenigot and Tetford, the scarp face of the chalk is wooded. More commonly it is in arable or grazing use, and on the very steepest sections, fragments of unimproved grassland occur. Along the Rivers Bain, Lymn and Calceby Beck, valley floor marshes and alder carr woodlands are common. Moving southward across the area, dense mixed hedgerows with fine mature oak, ash and sycamore trees become more frequent, and in the south-east, around Somersby, Harrington and Langton, there are modest country houses surrounded by parkland and mixed woodland. The numerous villages are sometimes rectangular in form, as at Tetford. They are generally built of brick, with churches of Spilsby Sandstone.

Tennyson was probably describing this view from above Tetford in his poem In Memoriam AHH.

As in other parts of the AONB, there are many prominent historic landscape features. Almost every hill or knoll has prehistoric barrows or earthworks; a Roman road stretches across the area from west to east; and there are many medieval moated sites and deserted villages, for example at Brinkhill and Fordington.

The south-eastern claylands

The south-eastern claylands.

South of Louth, much of the chalk ridge is blanketed in boulder clay and assumes a low, rounded form. Stretching from Little Cawthorpe to Welton le Marsh, this area is bounded on the west by the crest of the ridge, and on the east by minor roads along the line of the ancient trackway, Barton Street. Here the Wolds overlook and blend gently into the coastal plain, known locally as the Middle Marsh. There are relatively few villages, and the landscape has an empty, isolated feel, created partly by close proximity to the marshland.

The ridge is smooth and continuous except at South Thoresby where it is broken by the gentle valley of the Great Eau; and in the south where there are small dry valleys at Well Vale and Skendleby Psalter. The even slopes that extend down from the ridge are mainly in arable use but by far the strongest landscape elements are the simple, large blocks of oak-ash woodland that occur all along this edge and include Maltby, Haugham, Burwell, Willoughby and Welton Woods. Such extensive woodland occurs nowhere else in the Wolds and indeed this is one of the largest woodland concentrations in Lincolnshire as a whole. The area just outside the AONB is also well wooded, and this enhances the woodland character of the claylands.

Along Barton Street is a series of spring-line villages at the junction of the chalk and the clays. These small and generally unspoilt settlements include Little Cawthorpe, Muckton, South Thoresby and Welton le Marsh. At Kenwick and Claxby there are also country houses and parkland. Each village is marked by a prominent church tower, and formerly windmills were a traditional feature. In some areas, such as at Calceby and Welton le Wold, small-scale quarrying of the glacial sands and gravels has taken place. Along the top of the ridge, which in the south is probably both an ancient trackway and a Roman road, there are numerous archaeological remains from a variety of periods.

The chalk ridge becomes narrow and low in the south-east. Here it is viewed from the west, near Worlaby, where melt-water channels along the line of the Great Eau and its tributaries have breached the ridge.

Other aspects of landscape character

At a detailed level, the landscape character of the AONB is strongly influenced by the area's habitats, its archaeological and historic landscape features, and its buildings and settlements. There are many distinctive landscape features and elements that recur across the AONB and make a positive contribution not only to its scenic interest, but also to its conservation value. Such features include chalk grassland, wet valley woodland, ancient trackways, deserted medieval villages, and the vernacular architecture of many settlements. An understanding of the nature and distribution of these important landscape features may also assist in AONB management.

Ecology

The Lincolnshire Wolds landscape is strikingly different from most other limestone and chalk landscapes in the extent of arable cultivation, made possible by the area's fertile chalk and drift soils. The 'typical' chalk downland features of calcareous grassland and sheep walk were probably never widespread in the Wolds, due to the thinness of the chalk and the fact that much of the area is covered by glacial till. Such calcareous grasslands as did exist in any event had largely disappeared by the end of the parliamentary enclosures, 150 years ago [16]. For the same reasons, the scarp-face woodlands that are so characteristic of limestone and chalk landscapes such as the Cotswolds and Chilterns, generally do not occur in the Lincolnshire Wolds.

The surviving area of semi-natural habitat is very limited in extent, but nonetheless important, at least in a county and regional context. Chalk grassland does occur, and as might be expected, it is concentrated mainly on the steepest slopes. Although the greatest loss of chalk grassland took place during the parliamentary enclosures, further damage and decline has continued throughout the 20th century. Grassland has been lost partly to the plough, but also as a result of fertiliser applications, agricultural improvement, and scrubbing up of areas where grazing has not been maintained. Hence only around 50 ha of wholly unimproved chalk grassland now exist in the Wolds [17]. Most of these areas are protected by designation as Sites of Special Scientific Interest (SSSIs). There are other areas that, although degraded, would be capable of restoration, given appropriate management.

One of the best surviving grassland habitats of the Wolds lies within the road verges [18], both along the ancient trackways and the drove roads of the parliamentary period. As mentioned earlier, many of these roads are up to 20 m in width between hedgerows. The reasons why they are so wide are not fully understood but one possible explanation is that the Enclosure Commissioners were attempting to compensate for the loss of common grazing land. Until at least the early part of this century, the verges traditionally were in use for grazing. Today most are maintained by mowing. As fragments of often undisturbed, herb-rich ancient grassland, their flowers provide a wealth of colour and visual interest for the traveller through the Wolds.

The woodland cover of the Wolds is very limited: around 2.2 per cent, compared to a county average of around 4 per cent, and a national average of around 8 per cent. All woods are in private ownership; there are no Forestry Commission plantations.

On the chalk, there is very little native woodland. The sole example of a semi-natural chalk woodland is Tetford Wood, an ancient hazel-ash-wych elm woodland on the scarp face, just below the Bluestone Heath Road. Clumps and plantations of beech are common on the chalk, and on high ground. These are not native, and mainly represent 18th or 19th century plantings, but nonetheless make an important visual and ecological contribution.

Wet valley woodlands are found on heavy soils within the valleys. These occur in the north, for example around Stainton le Vale, where they are often of fairly recent origin, and in the south, for example along the Bain and the Lymn, where there are some superb unspoilt valley habitats. The character of these woodlands varies considerably according to the nature of the underlying rocks. In the north oak-ash stand types are most common. In the south, spring-line alder carr frequently lines the streams on the Kimmeridge Clay, while the drier Spilsby Sandstone on the slopes above supports stands of ash, sycamore and beech [18].

Wet valley woodlands are found throughout the AONB as here, where alder carr and valley mires occur along Ketsby Beck, a tributary of the Great Eau.

The most extensive woodlands, however, are those on the heavy calcareous clay soils of the south-east, which were less attractive to agriculture. Many of these oak-ash-hazel woodlands are of ancient origin [19] and are designated as SSSIs or Lincolnshire Trust for Nature Conservation reserves. One of the finest examples, just on the edge of the AONB, is Hoplands Wood, where a traditional coppice-with-standards management system has been reintroduced.

Other important habitat types within the Wolds include the hedgerows, the valley marshes, and the river corridors. Although most hedgerows are of 18th or 19th century origin and are almost pure hawthorn, it is still possible to distinguish the older, mixed hedgerows at parish boundaries and within the pre-enclosure landscapes that surround many villages. Valley marshes and mires occur where permeable rocks meet underlying impervious clays. For example in the glacial overflow valley at Swaby there is calcareous marsh; while acid valley mires occur near Donington on Bain on the Spilsby Sandstone.

The water quality of the rivers is generally good. Both the northern chalk streams such as Waithe Beck, and the more acidic waters of the Rivers Bain and Lymn support rich marginal and aquatic habitats [20].

Archaeology and heritage

The Lincolnshire Wolds hold a considerable legacy of archaeological and historic landscape features. Ancient trackways exist in other parts of the country, but seldom are they so well-preserved, or so important in helping to explain the development of the landscape. Running along the ridges and the former cliff line, through often empty landscapes, with wide views, one can vividly imagine their use by early peoples for travel and defensive purposes. The east-west salters' roads are also of considerable historical interest.

Most archaeologists and historians agree that the Wolds demonstrate a particular wealth of interest from a variety of periods. Analysis of prehistoric and Roman remains by aerial photography of cropmarks [21] shows a concentration of sites on the drift-free land of the plateaux and ridges of the Lincolnshire Wolds. A second group of sites occurs along spring lines. Most of the surviving long and round barrows in Lincolnshire are in the Wolds. From later periods there is also a rich variety of interest. The Lincolnshire Wolds contain one of the highest concentrations of deserted medieval villages in England [8, 12]. There are around 220 such sites in Lincolnshire as a whole, of which at least 40 occur in the Wolds. In the south-east, medieval moated sites on the heavy clay soils are common.

Deserted medieval villages can be located either through upstanding remains or through aerial photography.

Neolithic and Bronze age barrows such as this round barrow at Burgh Top are very common landmarks within the Wolds. Hill top barrows are often marked by trees.

This rich archaeological resource may be partly due to good survival rates and the fact that archaeological remains show up most readily on light soils. Nonetheless, the interest is considerable. One of the most important aspects of the area's archaeological heritage is its relatively high degree of visibility. Unlike many other parts of the country, where the history of human habitation is hidden from view, it is quite prominent in the Wolds. Some of most obvious features include the tumuli along High Street; the long barrows that line the ridge-top roads in the south-east; and the many deserted medieval villages, such as Cadeby, West Wykeham, Calcethorpe and Fordington, commonly sited on open hillsides above small chalk streams.

Buildings and settlement

The Lincolnshire Wolds AONB is not distinguished by a unified pattern of building materials or styles [22]. A variety of building stones, together with brick, have always been used in the area's churches, villages and farmsteads. Nonetheless, there are many fine features that make a positive contribution to the area's landscape character.

Chalk is a poor building stone, except for the tougher Totternhoe Beds. It was once used fairly widely for churches, farms and cottages and was employed in the construction of Louth Abbey. However its generally weak and crumbling structure meant that, where possible, other building stone or brick was preferred.

In the north-west, the Claxby Ironstone and the Tealby Limestone were quarried and used as building materials. The ironstone can be seen at Nettleton, where the buildings are a rich ochre in colour; while at Tealby and Walesby

In the north-west, the ironstone forms a handsome building material for villages such as Nettleton. However, use is confined to the small area around the local quarries.

the paler limestone is in use. These materials have helped to create the distinctive landscape character of the north-west scarp.

In the south, the Spilsby Sandstone, a form of greensand, is the usual material for churches and other public buildings. Like the chalk, it is often too weak to be a good building stone. Alec Clifton-Taylor, writing of the churches around Horncastle, says that if "they had more strength, these Lincolnshire churches would be among the most beguiling of all the English greensand buildings" [23].

Indeed, despite the limitations of the building stone, the Wolds contain numerous attractive medieval churches, ranging from squat, square-towered Norman and early English styles, through to more ornate 14th and 15th century buildings founded upon the medieval wool wealth. Examples of the former can be seen at Somersby and Bag Enderby; and the latter at Nettleton and Walesby.

For domestic buildings, the most common materials are brick and render. There were in fact a number of local brickworks, sited where streams cut through the chalk to the clays. Brick was in use from the 14th century onwards; and in the 17th century pantiles were introduced. Initially imported from Holland, later they were manufactured locally and replaced thatch as the traditional roofing material for the area. A Dutch influence can still be seen today in some of the buildings of the Wolds. Although the area as a whole may not be of outstanding architectural interest, there is a great deal of good domestic architecture, and many buildings are listed.

The shape and form of the area's villages tend to vary between the northern and southern parts of the Wolds, perhaps reflecting their respective Saxon and Danish origins. In general, the north is characterised by simple, nucleated villages, while in the south a rectangular plan is found, with lanes enclosing a central area given up to cottages, farmhouses and home paddocks, as at Goulceby and Tetford [24]. There are also street villages such as

Brick and pantile are the most common domestic building materials in the AONB.

Skendleby and Ulceby in the south. The vast majority of the area's villages nestle in the valleys. They are small, quiet, and relatively unaffected by modern development — and therein lies their charm. The comparative lack of recent development is no doubt due in part to the Wolds' isolated location, but even the Louth to Bardney railway line that connected the area to Lincoln from 1876 to 1951, did not bring significant development pressures

[25]. The only area where major new building has occurred is near Binbrook, where extensive housing was built to serve the airfield.

As mentioned earlier, the Wolds were never characterised by large or wealthy estates, with a few notable exceptions. Nevertheless there are some gracious but generally modest Tudor and Georgian country houses. A few of these have interesting gardens and parkland: for example Thorganby Hall, South Ormsby Hall, and Harrington Hall, which has links with Tennyson. There are also many fine Victorian farmsteads.

Overall character

Together, all these separate dimensions — visual, ecological, historical, and architectural — combine to give the Wolds a unique and distinctive landscape character. As we have seen, this character shows local variations. The north-west scarp, with its outward aspect, is perhaps the most dramatic landscape. The chalk wolds, which cover the largest area, form a more subtle landscape, dominated by agriculture. This landscape is distinguished by its internal contrasts and by its important archaeological features. The ridges and valleys of the south-west have an enormously complex physiography, and this is reflected in a marked diversity of scenery and habitats. The south-eastern claylands form a simpler and more wooded landscape, which shows strong links with the Middle Marsh below.

Overall, though, the Wolds have a clear and unified identity, recognised both locally and nationally, for example in writings about the area. In the next chapter we explore how the Wolds landscape has been perceived and valued, in the past and in the present day.

Early writings about the landscape

There are relatively few early records of how the Lincolnshire Wolds landscape was perceived, although the area has long had a clear identity as the main upland within the county. Few of the 16th and 17th century travellers such as John Leland and Celia Fiennes seem to have visited the Wolds, and descriptions of the landscape prior to the parliamentary enclosures are comparatively rare.

One of the first impressions of the Wolds comes from Daniel Defoe, who travelled through the area around the turn of the 18th century. He considered the landscape between Caistor, Spilsby and Horncastle to be unremarkable except for its stock-rearing, and noted that "all this country is employ'd in husbandry, in breeding and feeding innumerable droves and flocks of cattle and sheep" [26]. Later in the century, in 1799, the agricultural improver Arthur Young reported a bleak and heath-like landscape with "warren for thirty miles from Spilsby to beyond Caistor" [27].

By the early 19th century, a complete transformation had occurred as a result of the enclosures. Great pride was expressed in the productivity of the land. William Cobbett, in his *Rural Rides* of 1830, described the Lincolnshire Wolds with enthusiasm:

"This is a very fine corn country: chalk at bottom: stony near the surface in some places: here and there a chalk-pit in the hills: the shape of the ground somewhat like that of the broadest valleys in Wiltshire; but the fields not without fences as they are there: fields from fifteen to forty acres: the hills not downs, as in Wiltshire; but cultivated all over. The houses white and thatched, as they are in all chalk countries. The valley at Scamblesby has a little rivulet running down it, just as in all the chalk countries. The land continues nearly the same to Louth, which lies in a deep dell, with beautiful pastures on the surrounding hills" [28].

A similar view as voiced by J A Clarke writing in the *Journal of the Royal Agricultural Society* in 1852. He declared that:

"no portion of the ground has been allowed to remain (as on the Downs of southern England) a tract of sheepwalks in its primitive vegetation of heath and fern, but the highest parts are all in tillage and the whole length of the Wolds is intersected by neat whitethorn hedges, the solitary furze bush appearing only where a roadside or plantation offers an uncultivated space" [29].

Alfred Lord Tennyson, in his *Northern Farmer* poems, also recorded the energy and thoroughness with which the improvements had been achieved, for instance through the words of an old man, who on his death bed proudly remembers the reclamation of Thorganby Warren:

"Dubbut looäk at the waäste: theer warn't not feäd for a cow;
Nowt at all but bracken an' fuzz, an' looäk at it now —
Warn't worth nowt a haäcre, an' now theer's ots o' feäd
Fourscore yows upon it an' some on it doon in seäd."

Literary and artistic associations

Tennyson, in fact, was born at Somersby within the Lincolnshire Wolds and lived in the area until he was 28. He spent much time among the country people and walking the valleys and wolds above Somersby. The landscapes of Lincolnshire were certainly a source for much of his poetry. His memories of the area are clearly reflected in many of his works, although he seldom refers directly to the Lincolnshire Wolds [30].

For example, in *In Memorium AHH*, he is probably describing his farewell to the Wolds, which he left in 1837. The poem gives a strong sense of contrast between the bare tops of the chalk and the intimate sandstone landscapes below:

"Calm and deep peace on this high wold,
      And on these dews that drench the furze,
      And all the silvery gossamers
That twinkle into green and gold:

Calm and still light on yon great plain
      That sweeps with all its autumn bowers,
      And crowded farms and lessening towers,
To mingle with the bounding main."

Again, in *The Lady of Shalott* Tennyson conjures up a landscape that reflects the Wolds of his childhood:

"On either side the river lie
Long fields of barley and of rye
That clothe the wold and meet the sky;
And through the field the road runs by
To many-tower'd Camelot."

The Wolds also provided the setting for many other poems. For instance, Harrington Hall was the home of Rosa Baring, who inspired one of Tennyson's best-known poems, *Maud*:

"Come into the garden,
Maud, I am here at the gate alone,
And the woodbine spices are wafted abroad,
and the musk of the rose is blown."

Lincolnshire Landscape *by Peter De Wint (reproduced with kind permission of Lincolnshire County Council: Usher Gallery, Lincoln).*

The brook that flows through Somersby was a well-known haunt of Alfred and his brothers and it seems likely that his poem *The Brook* was influenced by childhood memories:

"By thirty hills I hurry down
Or slip between the ridges,
By twenty thorpes, a little town,
and half a hundred bridges,
Till last by Philip's farm I flow
to join the brimming river,
For men may come and men may go,
But I go on forever."

The Wolds landscape in the mid-19th century was also an inspiration to the well-known English landscape painter, Peter de Wint (1784–1849). Born in Staffordshire of Dutch and Scottish descent, de Wint married a Lincolnshire woman, and rustic Lincolnshire landscapes at the time of the enclosures were one of his favourite subjects. *A Lincolnshire Landscape* (subtitled *Lincolnshire Cornfield near Horncastle*) depicts the harvest in progress on the crest of the Wolds, with distant views of Lincoln Vale. Another view, *Harvest Field*, shows the rolling, hummocky face of the Wolds escarpment from the plain below. Both these scenes capture the atmosphere of the Wolds and reinforce the point that much of their attraction relies upon the views into and out of the area.

Contemporary perceptions

Since the turn of the 20th century, the popularity of the Lincolnshire Wolds has grown enormously. This is due in part to the area's associations with Tennyson, but also reflects the general growth in the popularity of chalk downland landscapes. A third factor is the increase in rural recreation. As large sections of the population gained access to private transport, the Wolds came to be recognised as touring and walking country unsurpassed within Lincolnshire.

James John Hissey, writing in 1898, describes a tour of the Wolds that took in the Tennyson country of Somersby and Harrington:

"From Harrington we returned to Horncastle by a roundabout route, passing through South Ormsby and Tetford, a route that led us through the heart of the wild Wolds, and gave us a good insight into its varied and characteristic scenery. A very enjoyable drive it proved, down dale and over hill, past many-tinted woods, gorgeous in their autumn colouring, through sleepy hamlets, and across one little ford, with a footbridge at the side for pedestrians, with the rounded hills bounding our prospect on every hand. Now the hills would be a wonderful purple-gray in cloud shadow, anon a brilliant golden green as the great gleams of sunshine raked their sloping sides, lighting them up with a warm glory that hardly seemed of this world, so ethereal did they make the solid landscape look." [31].

Later, in the 1930s, Rushworth wrote of the Wolds: "To stand anywhere on the eastern edges... and to see the great river Humber come sweeping past the Yorkshire bank... or to look southward beyond the exquisitely graceful spire of Louth parish church... is a sight seldom equalled and spreads a panorama before the eyes as extensive and varied as a view from a mountain top." [32].

This popularity has lasted through to the present day, and was one of the main reasons for the area's designation as an AONB in 1973, with the strong support of the local branch of the Council for the Protection of Rural England. Except around Somersby, the Wolds are not a major tourist destination, but they are a much-valued aesthetic and recreational resource. The visual contrast between the airy uplands and the valleys and spires below continues to give inspiration to contemporary painters such as Tom Brooker and David Cuppleditch. The Wolds are widely

used for walking and nature study, for example along the Viking Way long distance footpath. The wide-verged roads offer leisurely motoring and splendid views of quiet, unspoilt countryside — an increasingly scarce resource in Britain today.

In 1990, the Wolds formed a setting for the Booker Prize-winning novel *Possession* by A S Byatt [33]. Her description of arrival in the area gives a marvellous picture of the Wolds landscape:

"The wolds of Lincolnshire are a small surprise... The valleys are deep and narrow, some wooded, some grassy, some ploughed. The ridges run sharply across the sky, always bare. The rest of the large, sleepy country is marsh or fen or flat farmed plain. These slightly rolling hills appear to be folded out of the surface of the earth, but that is not the case; they are part of a dissected tableland. The villages are buried in the valleys, at the end of blind funnels." [33].

Towards Lincoln from Fuletby *by Tom Brooker (reproduced with kind permission of the artist).*

As the purpose of AONB designation is to conserve the natural beauty of the landscape, it is important to have an understanding of how the landscape has changed in the recent past, how it may change in future, and the effects that change may have upon its landscape character and qualities. Not all change is detrimental; indeed it is a natural part of a landscape's evolution.

Change this century

Compared to many other parts of the country, the Lincolnshire Wolds have experienced remarkably little landscape change this century. The basic structure and character of the landscape today are still very much as they were when the enclosures were completed in the 1830s.

The overriding influence has probably been agricultural intensification. During the Second World War much grassland was ploughed up for arable production, and it is likely that this led to the loss of many of those areas of unimproved grassland that had survived the enclosures. In the post-war period this trend has continued, as the use of chemical fertilisers has revolutionised the farming system, for example, by permitting continuous arable cropping. County-wide figures give some indication of the scale of conversion from mixed to arable farming that has taken place. In 1905, 33 per cent of land was in permanent pasture. By 1945, this had fallen to around 25 per cent, and by 1966 to 16 per cent [18].

Although the basic structure of the landscape has not changed dramatically since the mid-1800s, agricultural intensification has encouraged hedgerow removal.

At the same time greater use of large machinery and chemicals has encouraged hedgerow removal, although as the fields were already quite large, the effects of removal has not been as dramatic as elsewhere. Amalgamation of farm holdings, to create bigger, more economic units has also occurred. This in turn has led to the construction of large, new and sometimes visually intrusive farm buildings, and to the abandonment of some of the more remote farms and cottages. There has been a marked decline in population and local services. For example, it is estimated that between 1971 and 1989 over half the parishes within the AONB saw a net population decrease, while almost a third lost their local shop.

The Wolds represent the highest ground in eastern England between Kent and Yorkshire, and as such are a favoured location for telecommunications and defence installations. These communication dishes at Nob Hill near Donington on Bain are one of a number of installations that intrude upon the surrounding landscape.

Built development within the AONB has generally been fairly limited, due to the area's comparative isolation. During the Second World War, there were five airfields within the Wolds [34]. At the end of the war, most of these closed, although some, such as Ludford Magna, left a legacy of dereliction. At Binbrook, which became a permanent RAF base, substantial housing and military development occurred post-war. Radio and telecommunications masts have become prominent features on many hillsides. Some of these masts, such as that at Stenigot, are now of historic value as relics of the Second World War; but others, such as the cluster of masts along High Street near Caistor, are unsightly.

Mineral extraction and landfill have taken place in parts of the AONB, for example at Nettleton where chalk is quarried. Planning policies do however, generally discourage such development.

In those villages within easy reach of Lincoln and Grimsby, new infill housing has been built for use by commuters. Mineral and landfill development has taken place, especially on the chalk at the northern end of the AONB and on the glacial sands and gravels of the south-east. New and improved roads have also been built — notably the A16 bypass to the west of Louth, which cuts across the valley landscapes of the River Lud.

Prospects for future change

As the Lincolnshire Wolds is essentially a farmed landscape, changes in agricultural policy and support systems are likely to be the main source of future landscape change. The effects of European Community (EC) agricultural policy can already be seen in the growth of crops such as oil seed rape and linseed, which have brought new colours to a landscape previously dominated by winter wheat and barley.

A further, major change is in the pipeline at present, with the introduction of a new EC Set-Aside scheme from 1992–1993. In order to qualify for EC arable area payments, most farmers will need to take 15 per cent of their arable land out of production. Initially, the set-aside is to be rotational: land will either be left fallow or sown with a green cover crop. The effects on the countryside will be temporary, but even in the short term may be quite dramatic. Unsightly weed cover is one possibility. In the longer term, permanent set-aside (for example to pasture or woodland) may be introduced. The effects are difficult to predict, as details of this scheme are not yet available. However, the potential impact on the Lincolnshire landscape could be considerable.

In the longer term, the new EC Agro-Environmental Directive, which is likely to be passed soon, could bring further changes, towards agricultural extensification, organic farming, and community use of farmland. Again, it is too early to predict how this may affect the landscape.

Other land use changes are likely to be more modest in scale. The agricultural restructuring that took place in the post-war period left a fairly stable pattern of land holdings dominated by traditional, medium-sized owner-occupied farms, although there are more recent signs of an increase in smallholdings, and breakup of some large agricultural units. Widespread new farm building is no longer likely, as the grant-aid schemes for farm buildings have largely been discontinued. Arable intensification may continue in a modest way. This is confirmed by analysis of agricultural census data for 1984 to 1991, which show a continuing gradual decline in permanent grassland, from 12.1 per cent to 10.0 per cent.

However, positive changes are also taking place. The same agricultural census data show a slight expansion in the areas of rough grazing and woodland within the AONB. These trends probably reflect the new incentives that have become available for farm conservation since the early 1980s, including the original Set-Aside scheme, the Woodland Grant Scheme, and most recently the Countryside Stewardship scheme. The uptake for the Woodland Grant Scheme has been quite good, and has led to the creation of new small woodlands along the north-west scarp, around Louth, and on the claylands of the south-east. Countryside Stewardship has also been quite popular, with funds being targeted towards chalk

Positive landscape change is being achieved within the AONB through schemes such as Countryside Stewardship, with particular efforts being made to reinstate chalk grassland habitats.

grasslands, waterside landscapes, and historic landscapes. The local wildlife trust, the Lincolnshire Trust for Nature Conservation, is very active within the Wolds. It has acquired and manages eight nature reserves. It has also established a protected road verge scheme, in consultation with Lincolnshire County Council and landowners [35].

In relation to the built environment, it seems unlikely that there will be radical changes in the immediate future. Development pressures are perceived to be relatively low, and although the county and district councils are generally pro-development, special protection is given to the AONB. Any large-scale new development would almost certainly be directed away from the area.

Instead we are much more likely to see small-scale conversion of buildings in the countryside, and the development of new rural farm-based attractions, in line with structure plan policy to encourage farm diversification. In addition, the Lincolnshire Wolds are a pilot area for the Rural Development Commission's new countryside employment programme, which aims to provide employment for those leaving the agricultural sector. This will encourage new, small-scale enterprises in the countryside; but it is also designed to assist in environmental improvement. It may provide a welcome opportunity to conserve some of the fine Georgian and Victorian farm buildings that have fallen vacant in recent decades.

One area that will certainly see change is Binbrook airfield, where the RAF base recently closed and the site has been sold. The District Council originally prepared a planning brief for the guidance of developers and purchasers but this has been largely superseded by new proposals included in the West Lindsey Draft Local Plan. The plan proposes that the airfield should be allocated for employment use (for example business park or light industrial use) and suggests that some expansion of existing housing and community facilities might be appropriate as part of an overall scheme for redevelopment.

Elsewhere in the AONB, any new built development is likely to be fairly modest in scale. In relation to housing development, further infill will probably take place. Care will need to be taken to ensure that any visual impact upon surrounding countryside is satisfactorily contained, and that the choice of building materials and styles is sympathetic: some villages, such as Claxby and Wold Newton, have been adversely affected by inharmonious development in the past. Loose-knit villages such as Tetford are particularly vulnerable to new development, which could easily alter their special, open character. In villages close to the Viking Way, such as Walesby, parking and visitor pressures at peak periods may be a growing problem.

No major new road building is likely within the AONB, but several improvement schemes may affect the periphery. These include the A16 improvements along the eastern edge of the AONB, and the A46 Swallow bypass east of Caistor. Finally, some further expansion of mineral and landfill activity may be expected. Consents have been granted for chalk extraction at Nettleton and North Ormsby and for sand and gravel extraction at Donington on Bain and elsewhere. The effects of these developments, hopefully, should be fairly localised. In the longer term, large-scale mineral and landfill development is unlikely because of the limited local demand, and because of increasingly stringent groundwater protection policies, which may preclude waste disposal on chalk.

Potential threats to the AONB landscape

Not all landscape change constitutes a threat. As we have seen, some changes are a natural part of a landscape's evolution, and some are deliberate improvements brought about by positive planning and management. A 'threat' occurs only when some valued landscape attribute is damaged by change. Some threats are gradual, and hard to detect; others are more obvious. The degree of threat also depends upon the sensitivity to change or visual intrusion of a specific landscape type. For example, scarp face landscapes are inherently vulnerable since any change can be seen for miles.

Potential threats to the Lincolnshire Wolds landscape can broadly be classed into those arising from land use change, and those resulting from development. Land use changes result, primarily, from day-to-day decisions by landowners and land managers and as such are often outside the scope of the planning system. In contrast, new built developments are usually subject to planning controls, so any threats can be countered more readily.

Threats due to land use change

The cumulative effects of changes in land use and management are often slow and insidious. Arable intensification has led to gradual loss of the AONB's chalk grassland. Although the decline has now been more or less arrested, some of the remaining sites are suffering through lack of grazing, which is essential to the maintenance of their botanical interest. Unless they are grazed, the grasslands will tend to scrub up, and eventually become woodland. Also, some farmers have chosen to plant what they see as steep and unproductive slopes, again resulting in loss of the traditional grassland habitat.

Many of the small woodlands, copses and hedgerow trees of the Lincolnshire Wolds were planted in the 18th and 19th centuries, and are now over mature and unmanaged. Although they still form fine landscape features their effective lifespan will be very short unless positive management and renewal take place soon. The distinctive beech clumps that mark the hill crests throughout the area could all be lost within a remarkably short space of time. The hedgerow trees in some areas also show signs of disease and stress — which may be partly due to heavy fertiliser applications.

In parts of the AONB, there has been misguided tree planting within the wide grass verges of the ancient trackways and drove roads. This is not only out of keeping with their traditional character, but makes management of the verges difficult, and in the long term could obscure the characteristic hill top views. Views are already obscured in some areas by tall, A-shaped hedges, for example on the Rothwell estate; while at Clapgate Farm near Scamblesby a farmer has built a huge earthen enclosure for intensive cattle rearing. Although opinions may vary as to the merits of these particular schemes, they serve to illustrate how readily landscape character may be altered by changes in management practice.

There is growing concern, throughout the country, over depletion of groundwater resources, and the Wolds are no exception. The underlying Chalk and Spilsby Sandstone are aquifers, providing water supply for the coastal resort towns of Lincolnshire. In recent years, with drought conditions, there has also been a growing demand from farmers to abstract water by means of boreholes, for spray irrigation. It is now recognised that groundwater depletion is damaging wetlands, streams and river corridor habitats, especially around the southern and eastern edges of the Wolds [36]. The River Lud, for example, is affected. In some cases, these low flow effects may lead in turn to water quality problems, due to reduced dilution of effluent and farm run-off.

One of the most serious side-effects of agricultural intensification has been damage to, or loss of, the archaeological resource. The archaeological remains that show up as crop marks or surface features, all lie within the top layers of the soil. They are very vulnerable to deep ploughing, especially when permanent grassland is converted to arable use. It is estimated that in the last five years alone as many as two dozen deserted medieval village sites in Lincolnshire may have been affected in this way. Every effort should be made to avert any further such loss, especially within the AONB.

Valuable archaeological resources lying just beneath the surface can be damaged by deep ploughing and other agricultural practices. These earthworks at North Ormsby are probably connected with the village's ruined medieval abbey.

Golf course development may represent a threat to the AONB landscape, as this example at Louth suggests.

Lastly, golf course development on land that was previously in agricultural use is likely to represent a threat. New clubhouse facilities, evergreen planting and manicured fairways are often out of keeping with surrounding landscapes. Some examples of intrusive golf course development can already be seen in the valley landscapes near Louth. Golf courses may bring associated built development such as hotels and housing, and this is wholly inappropriate within an AONB.

Threats due to development

The Lincolnshire Wolds landscape is especially vulnerable to visual intrusion by any large-scale built development, because of its very open character and its extensive outward views. These views bring wide areas of the surrounding countryside within the 'visual envelope' of the Wolds, and increase their sensitivity. Development not only within the area, but on its periphery, could have significant, adverse impacts.

Although no major immediate development threats are known, it is important to highlight potential threats that could arise in future, and should be resisted. These include:

- any further, large-scale military or communications development, which may be seeking a site on high ground such as that of the Wolds;
- a new east coast motorway, which if developed might pass close to the west of the Wolds escarpment, bringing significant new development pressures;
- wind farm development, which could occur on the Wolds or the adjacent coastal plain, where wind speeds are high;
- nearby industrial development such as onshore oil and gas, power station or transmission line installations.

A vision for the future

The Countryside Commission encourages local authorities, landowners, and relevant government and voluntary bodies to take an active role in the management of AONB landscapes. One of the first steps is usually the preparation of an AONB management plan. The management plan offers an opportunity to set objectives and targets for conservation and enhancement of the AONB landscape as a whole. Ideally, it should also be designed to help reinforce the distinctive character of the AONB and its constituent landscape types. It should not only aim to counter the threats to the landscape that may rise from changing land use and built development, but should also identify positive opportunities for action.

There are already a great many initiatives in place that can contribute towards the management of the Lincolnshire Wolds landscape. These include the Woodland Grant Scheme, with its new Community Woodland Supplement for plantings close to towns; the Countryside Commission's Countryside Stewardship scheme and the Hedgerow Incentive Scheme; the local authorities' Countryside Management Project, which is achieving many small-scale landscape, recreation and access improvements; and the ongoing activities of bodies such as the Farming and Wildlife Advisory Group (FWAG), Lincolnshire Trust for Nature Conservation (LTNC), and the Rural Development Commission. What is needed is a plan to ensure that the considerable efforts and resources of these schemes and organisations are carefully directed towards common goals and priorities, to achieve the optimum effect, overall.

It will be the task of the Lincolnshire Wolds AONB Forum to take this initiative forward, but we hope that this landscape assessment will provide the foundation for the Forum's work. We set out below some of the issues that we regard as priorities to be addressed in any future management plan. We would stress that the management plan should be a creative, visionary document to guide the AONB landscape for the next 20 to 30 years. It should define clearly the respective roles of all of the different organisations and interests that have a part to play, and should indicate exactly where and how resources should be targeted.

For the AONB generally, the overall goal should be to conserve and enhance the distinctive landscape qualities of the Wolds, including the enormous views; the open sweeping landform and ridge-top routeways; the seasonally changing cropping patterns; and the deep, dramatic, wooded valleys. The following points are among the issues that a future management plan will need to tackle.

- Expansion of the area of chalk grassland is important. The Countryside Stewardship scheme and other appropriate mechanisms should be used to reconstruct the scarp face and road verge grasslands, and ensure their future management by grazing or mowing. This may require some removal of scrub woodland and inappropriate roadside plantings.

- Urgent attention should be given to the management and renewal of small woodlands, beech clumps and hedgerow trees. Here the main responsibility must lie with landowners, although the County Council, the Countryside Management Project, FWAG and LTNC can offer advice and assistance.

- New woodland planting should reinforce the pattern of existing woodlands. Favoured areas for planting might include the valley landscapes throughout the area, and the south-eastern claylands. Grant aid for new woodland planting should be positively directed towards these areas. For example, with the agreement of the Forestry Commission, the Community Woodland Supplement might be targeted to the valleys west of Louth.

- Action should be taken to identify, conserve and reinstate hedgerows, especially the old, mixed, pre-enclosure hedgerows. Here the Countryside Commission's Hedgerow Incentive Scheme has a special role to play.

- Waterside landscapes are an undervalued resource within the AONB. They occur particularly along the eastern and southern fringes of the AONB. The Countryside Stewardship Scheme offers scope to re-establish flower-rich meadows along the area's streams. The issue of low flow effects needs to be addressed in consultation with the National Rivers Authority.

- It is important to combat any further loss of the AONB's special archaeological resource. This may be achieved through a programme to advise and inform landowners of the sensitivity of this resource. Public access to, and interpretation of, the area's many sites and monuments may also be encouraged as part of the Countryside Management Project and schemes for farm diversification.

- There should be a general presumption against golf course development proposals within the AONB, unless it can be demonstrated that they contribute to, and enhance, the special landscape qualities of the area. Other new recreational uses should be low-key, and encourage quiet enjoyment of the countryside.

- New built development and farm building conversions within the area should be sensitively designed and handled. Planning authorities, in their development control policies, should recognise and respect the distinctive characters of different parts of the AONB, and should ensure that new development within villages is contained visually. There is no place within the AONB, or around its periphery, for large-scale, intrusive housing, road, minerals or industrial development.

The management plan should also look carefully at the specific threats and opportunities that occur within each landscape character area, and consider how the diversity of the AONB's landscapes may be maintained and heightened, by directing particular actions to particular areas.

For example, on the north-west scarp, grazing reinstatement will be a priority, and the special sensitivity to change of the scarp face should be noted. Within the chalk wolds landscape, the renewal of the characteristic beech clumps and the hedgerow trees is most urgent. There are also great opportunities to extend and accentuate the pattern of valley woodlands. Within the ridge and valley landscapes of the south-west, waterside landscapes, parkland and old mixed hedgerows are among the most distinctive landscape features, and their conservation and restoration should be priorities. The south-eastern claylands, with their heavier soils and existing wooded character, may be targeted for major new planting.

AONB designation

The value attached to the Lincolnshire Wolds landscape has already been demonstrated by the area's designation as an AONB in 1973, which places it among the most prized landscapes in England. Broadly, the designation means that:

- the landscape is a resource of national importance, for reasons of rarity, variety or representativeness;
- it is of high aesthetic quality, with specially pleasing patterns and combinations of landscape features;
- in addition to its scenic qualities, it includes other notable conservation interests, such as features of outstanding geological, wildlife, heritage or architectural interest;
- there is a consensus of both professional and public opinion as to its importance.

In our view, it is quite clear that the Lincolnshire Wolds AONB meets these criteria. The area has a combination of features that is unusual, or even unique in a national context. Visually, it is a delight to visit, and its aesthetic qualities are matched by a special concentration of geological and heritage features of national importance. The area has significant cultural associations, notably the link with Tennyson, and is highly valued by local residents and visitors. We summarise below the special qualities of the Lincolnshire Wolds that make the area an outstanding landscape.

Outstanding qualities

A unique physiography

The physical geography of the Lincolnshire Wolds is unusual and fascinating. The Wolds form the only upland landscape of eastern England; and nowhere else in Britain has a chalkland landscape been so extensively modified by glaciation. The topography alone is one of the area's greatest assets. It gives a sense of surprise on arrival, and creates views that are unparalleled within the region. The ancient coastal cliffs, glacial spillways and ponded-lake systems that helped to form the Wolds are unique, and create a strong and distinctive sense of contrast between the tops and valleys.

A scenic, working landscape

Unlike many other AONBs, the high scenic quality of the Lincolnshire Wolds depends almost entirely upon the area's use for agriculture. Much of its charm is derived from the seasonally changing field and cropping patterns;

the quiet scenes of farming activity; and the traditional villages and farmsteads in brick and pantile. The influence of the underlying geology and soils on land use is very marked, and acts to reinforce the contrast between the high wolds and the vales of the south and east. This contrast is further heightened by the pattern of enclosure landscapes and drove roads on high ground, with more ancient habitats and landscapes below.

A major archaeological resource

The Wolds have been described as "a prime archaeological environment" [21] — a status that needs to be more widely recognised. Often, the archaeological interest can be readily seen and makes a major contribution to landscape character. The Wolds are crossed by ancient trackways with romantic names. They have a rich legacy of prehistoric sites, and are especially distinguished for their concentration of deserted medieval villages. A classic parliamentary enclosure landscape has been overlain, so that in most areas there is a wealth of historic landscape features from different periods.

There is a rich legacy of prehistoric sites within the Wolds. The ancient trackways have many historic associations and are very popular as touring routes.

A valued cultural landscape

Finally, the Wolds landscape is of immense popular appeal. As the boyhood home of Tennyson, it features in many of his works. This landscape offered inspiration to 19th century artists and has risen to popularity in the 20th century, particularly, as fine walking and touring country. The high value that is placed on the area is evidenced in writings, in the work of contemporary painters, and in the active support for the AONB designation that has been shown by many local groups.

Conclusion

Clearly, the Lincolnshire Wolds AONB is a landscape of national importance. Its scenery is subtle and complex, with a specially fascinating history. The more one comes to know and understand the area, the greater its appeal.

This short report, has aimed to describe, succinctly, the evolution of the Wolds landscape, and to suggest sources for further study. The present-day landscape character of the area has been analysed, recognising that there are local variations, and many different facets to that character. Study of the perceptions of travellers, writers and artists who have visited the Wolds has yielded insight into how and why the landscape is valued. Prospects for landscape change have been reviewed. This has shown that there are a number of threats to the AONB landscape; but it has also identified many positive opportunities for conservation

and enhancement of the AONB. Key issues that will need to be addressed in future have been highlighted.

The most challenging work is still to come: namely the preparation and implementation of a creative, visionary management plan to guide the AONB landscape for the next 20 to 30 years. This will be the responsibility of the local authorities, land owners and managers, wildlife and amenity bodies who form part of the Lincolnshire Wolds Forum. We hope that they will be inspired, like generations before them, by the Lincolnshire Wolds landscape itself: where landform, geology, soils, habitats and patterns of previous human usage all lend pointers for the future, but there is scope for new landscape features, too.

The timeless, yet adaptable qualities of the Lincolnshire Wolds landscape are very aptly summed up by a modern-day writer, in *Country Life*. Describing the view from the top of the Wolds, he says:

"From... the Bluestone Heath Road... one best appreciates the variety of the Wolds scenery: smoothly rounded hills, green except in high summer when they are yellow, like a vast Van Gogh canvas, with oil seed rape; and long stretches of tableland... sometimes in shallow folds, behind shelter belts mainly of beech... above valleys of lazy streams along which the villages lie." [37].

The Wolds are essentially a working landscape. Geology, soils, seasonal rhythms and the farming calendar are the main influences on the appearance of the land.

REFERENCES

1. Lindsey County Council (1971), *The Lincolnshire Wolds Area of Outstanding Natural Beauty: Statement of Intent*, Lindsey County Council, Louth.

2. Kent, P (1980), *British Regional Geology: Eastern England from the Tees to the Wash*, HMSO, London.

3. Swinnerton, H H and P E Kent (1976), *The geology of Lincolnshire*, Lincolnshire Naturalists' Union, Lincoln.

4. Robinson, D N (1975), '*Geology and scenery*', in E J Gibbons, *The Flora of Lincolnshire*, Lincolnshire Naturalists' Union, Lincoln *op cit*.

5. Straw, A (1961), 'Drifts, meltwater channels and ice margins in the Lincolnshire Wolds', in *Transactions of the Institute of British Geographers* 29, 115–128.

6. Straw, A (1966), 'The development of the middle and lower Bain valley', in *Transactions of the Institute of British Geographers* 40, 145–154.

7. Straw, A (1969), *Lincolnshire soils*, Lincolnshire Natural History Brochure No 3, Lincolnshire Naturalists' Union, Lincoln.

8. Everson, P L et al (1991), *Change and continuity: Rural settlement in North-West Lincolnshire*, HMSO, London.

9. May, J (1976), 'Prehistoric Lincolnshire', in *History of Lincolnshire Volume 1*, History of Lincolnshire Committee, Lincoln.

10. Rogers, A (1985), *A History of Lincolnshire*, Phillimore, Chichester.

11. Platts, G (1985), 'Land and People in Medieval Lincolnshire', in *History of Lincolnshire Volume IV*, History of Lincolnshire Committee, Lincoln.

12. Beresford, M and J G Hurst (eds) (1989), *Deserted medieval villages*, Alan Sutton, Gloucester.

13. Doughty, P S (1965), 'The rabbit in Lincolnshire: a short history' in *Journal of the Scunthorpe Museum Society* 2, 15–23.

14. Russell E and R C (1985), *Old and new landscapes in the Horncastle area*, Lincolnshire County Council, Lincoln.

15. Darby, H C (1952), 'The Lincolnshire Wolds', in *Lincolnshire Historian* 9, 315–324.

16. Gibbons, E J (1975), 'The flora of the major habitats' in E J Gibbons, *The Flora of Lincolnshire*, Lincolnshire Naturalists' Union, Lincoln.

17. Blake, C (1990), *Lincolnshire chalk grassland survey*, unpublished report for the Nature Conservancy Council, Peterborough.

18. Smith, A E (1969), *Nature conservation in Lincolnshire*, Lincolnshire Naturalists' Union, Lincoln.

19. Hughes, D P (1988), *Lincolnshire inventory of ancient woodlands*, unpublished report for the Nature Conservancy Council, Peterborough.

20. Reid, S and J Ostler (1988), *River Bain survey*, unpublished report for the Nature Conservancy Council, Peterborough.

21. Jones, D (1988), 'Aerial reconnaissance and prehistoric and Romano-British archaeology in northern Lincolnshire', in *Lincolnshire history and archaeology* 23, 5–29.

22. Miller, T and D Robinson (1989), 'Geology and building materials', in N Pevsner and J Harris (eds), *Buildings of England: Lincolnshire*, Penguin, Harmondsworth.

23. Clifton-Taylor, A (1987), *The pattern of English building*, Faber and Faber, London.

24. Barley, M W (1972), *Lincolnshire and the Fens*, E P Publishing, Wakefield.

25. Ludlam, A J and W B Herbert (1987), *The Louth to Bardney branch*, Oakwood Press, Oxford.

26. Defoe, D (1699–1731), *Travels through England and Wales*, Volume 2.

27. Young, A (1799), *General view of the agriculture of the county of Lincolnshire*.

28. Cobbett, W (1830), *Rural rides*, Volume 2.

29. Clarke, J A (1852), *Journal of the Royal Agricultural Society*.

30. Furlong, P (1989), *Aesthetic East Lindsey*, Imp-Art Publications, Grimoldy.

31. Hissey, J J (1898), *Over Fen and Wold*, Macmillan, London.

32. Rushworth, N A (1938), 'Lincolnshire', in S P B Mais and T Stephenson (eds), *Lovely Britain*, Odhams.

33. Byatt, A S (1990), *Possession: A romance*, Vintage, London.

34. Blake, R et al (1984), *The Airfields of Lincolnshire since 1912*, Midland Counties Publication, Leicester.

35. Crooks, S E (1989), *Nature reserves handbook*, Lincolnshire and South Humberside Trust for Nature Conservation, Alford.

36. National Rivers Authority Anglian Region (1992), *Louth coastal catchment management plan Consultation Report*, National Rivers Authority, Peterborough.

37. Christian, R (1986), 'Tranquillity in Tennyson country: the Lincolnshire Wolds', in *Country Life*, 25 December, 2038–2040.

ACKNOWLEDGEMENTS

Thanks are due to all of the many organisations and individuals who provided invaluable information, comment and local knowledge of the Lincolnshire Wolds landscape. We are especially grateful for the assistance of David N Robinson of the Lincolnshire Trust for Nature Conservation, who very generously gave or lent many personal papers and helped with interpretation of the area's geology and glaciation.

Many others also lent help and support, notably Judith Feline of the Countryside Commission's Eastern Regional Office, and Ray Taylor of the Recreational Services Department of Lincolnshire County Council, who jointly steered the study, and organised a special meeting of the Lincolnshire Wolds Forum, at which a draft report was presented and discussed.

Chris Kerry and Angela Baker of Cobham Resource Consultants dealt patiently and efficiently with word processing, maps and illustrations.

The study team comprised Julie Martin, Mike Habermehl and Jackie Hunt of Cobham Resource Consultants, and Dr Peter Howard of the University of Plymouth, who advised on landscape perceptions. All photographs are by Mike Williams, except those on pages 5, 16, 17, 23, which are by Lincolnshire County Council.